VERSUS: An American Architect's Alternatives

1985

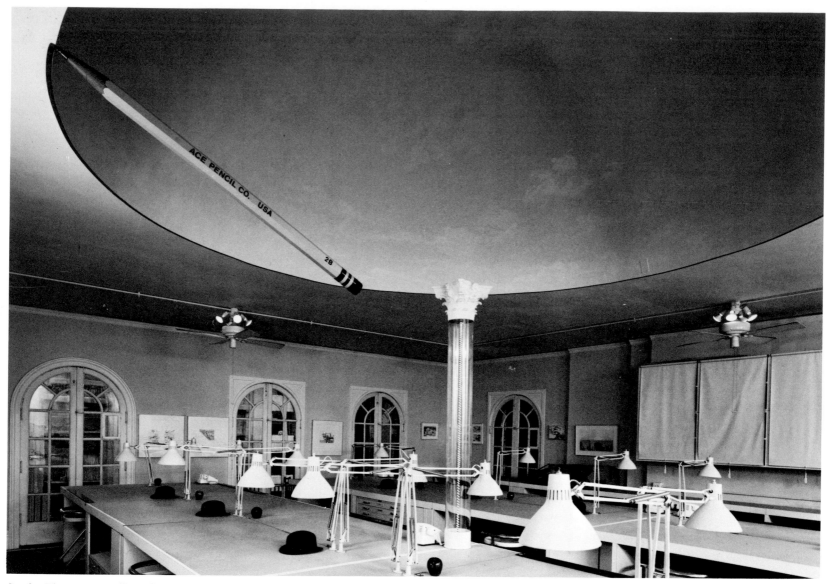

Stanley Tigerman's studio, Chicago, Illinois, 1977

VERSUS

An American Architect's Alternatives by Stanley Tigerman

With essays by Ross Miller and Dorothy Metzger Habel

RIZZOLI
NEW YORK

All drawings are by Stanley Tigerman unless otherwise designated.

Published in the United States of America in 1982 by
RIZZOLI INTERNATIONAL PUBLICATIONS, INC.
712 Fifth Avenue, New York, NY 10019

LC: 81-86435
ISBN: hardcover 0-8478-0429-1   paperback: 0-8478-0433-X

Edited by Brenda Gilchrist
Designed by Abby Goldstein
Set in type by Candice Odell
Printed and bound by Interstate Book Manufacturers, Inc.,
Olathe, Kansas

Contents

For Margaret, Judson and Tracy

Introduction

For the past several years I have become increasingly aware (and ultimately quite supportive) of the reason why no archetypal Jewish Mother ever boasts of "my son, the architect." Typically the quote refers to "my son, the lawyer" or, equally often, "my son, the doctor." So why does it never come out as "my son, the architect"? Just what is it about architecture that precludes it from inclusion in the cultural tradition of such a signal figure as the Jewish Mother?

It is my contention that ideality and perpetuity—the bookends of architectural aspiration—have no place in the temporal thought contained within the tradition of Judaism. I thereby intend in this book to confront these joint goals of ideality and perpetuity and to propose that architecture can hold a dialectical position within the dualistic tradition of simultaneity. This argumentative attitude I realize stands outside the mainstream Zeitgeist theory of architecture.

Ever since Andrea Palladio wrote *I Quattro Libri dell' Architettura* in 1570 architects who have been their own biographers have used their work to suggest (as Palladio himself did) one, right, legitimate way of making architecture. The morality (or chutzpah) this implies, that an architect molds his epoch rather than reflects it, intrigues me since in my own work I am not at all interested in finding a new, right way of making—or, for that matter, even looking at—things. But the nature of the times involved—from 1960 to 1980—was not particularly conducive to the ennoblement of the human spirit, at least not in America. And in many respects this book is about America itself—an America that falls from grace yet is as American as Philip Roth, Woody Allen and Kurt Vonnegut. It is not about the values of Thoreau and Emerson, or of Sullivan and Wright, though it does allude to Jeffersonian democracy. It is also not about the American dream in the sense of apple pie, motherhood and other lesser known metaphors for Platonic perfection, but neither is it about the nightmare of American civilization. What the book is about is one small, hand-held, two-sided mirror that reflects the times in architectural terms; and it proposes the theory that having more than one attitude in architecture is not necessarily as arbitrary as is normally thought.

Architects more often than not are trained to perceive of themselves as the "beckoning fair ones" of civilization. This can be seen in their avowed mission to monumentalize man's noble spirit (Mies van der Rohe once called architecture "the will of an epoch translated into space") and in their attitude, implicit throughout history, that they can actually change the nature of the times by what they build. Their concepts, when identified as being Futurist, convey the idea of perpetuity. There is something in these notions indicative of idealized forms if not, indeed, idealized worlds. My purpose here in recounting the 1960s and the 1970s through my work is to show that a career, uneven and faulty, to be sure, but a career of sorts nonetheless, can be wrought out of the most difficult of times and that architecture is not just a matter of finding the one, right, legitimate way of making anything. In fact, what my nine chapters (or books, if you like, since each contains work significantly different from that in the others) really represent are nine rather different careers viewed stylistically, socially and perceptually in the time span of twenty years. One might reasonably ask: Isn't there something Svengali-like (or at least Dr. Doolittle-like) in this rolling with the punches? Worse: Isn't there something unprofessional in capitalizing on the times rather than molding them to create a more perfect state of being? I happen to think not. My work in fact represents the struggle to come to grips with two opposing points of view: with a kind of talmudic logic I have focused both on my training in the lan-

guage of perfection and on my perverse desire to confront the idealized conditions of that training. There are no lessons to be learned with respect to emulation since I hardly represent an ideal role model, especially if synthesis is the goal.

What is of possible interest, however, is my belief that architects have a function in society to reflect their times through their clients, even if these times seem to change quickly. It has long been obvious to me that clients are far less pretentious than architects, and thus capable of more accurately reflecting the varying spirit of the times. Also of possible interest—as a result of recording my work in the way I have done—is the inference that there exists an "American" architecture, which, while not ideal or idealized, is nonetheless real and true and very "American" indeed. This is not to imply that imperfection, crassness and the cheap shot are wonderful, any more than that trendiness and fashion are necessarily desirable. But all these elements are "American," the cleansed directions advocated by the international architectural zealotry of the last fifty years notwithstanding.

In his book *Morality and Architecture*, the critic David Watkin scans architectural "correctness" and the question of the morality of the Zeitgeist theory of epochal representation. There is another kind of architectural morality seldom written about, however, that deals with architecture as a matter of service—service to the client. If clients and situations differ from project to project, it follows that architecture can be particularized to these sets of unique conditions. To extend this idea further, architecture can also provide a kind of commentary on the specifics of the times. The Zeitgeist theory in architecture, on the other hand, holds that generalizing is what finally best represents a particular epoch.

All this is what my book is about, since it is what my architecture has increasingly been about for the twenty years represented here. In the end the work is much more like Philip Roth than Plato—but so was America vintage 1960–80. It is clearly not avant-garde, for which I take the credit and blame. I carefully navigated my way around the shoals of seductive sirens searching for the central tune of the moment, which, when I discovered it, was what I played, at least for a time. In seeking acceptance, I changed the tune with regularity. Finally I managed to distance myself from this musical show through the use of the one idea that had sustained me on my odyssey: architecture as a responsive set or chords to the many melodies of the times.

This book is thus about the nature of struggle—not the outcome, for there are no real winners or losers here. What exists for me now is simply the representation of that ongoing struggle.

As each successive chapter moves farther and farther away from maintaining single overriding attitudes toward specific buildings, or toward buildings in general, and closer and closer to a joint representation of opposing values within a building, clarity gives way to ambiguity and Platonic ideality to Aristotelian argumentation. Indeed the very tradition of synthesis is gradually eroded, suggesting the greater power of the juxtaposition of thesis and antithesis. This point of view may well be roundly criticized within the continuum of architectural tradition begun in Hellenic times and reinstituted in the Renaissance.

It is not my conscious aim to be controversial, however. As I hope to make clear, I believe it is within the realm of architecture to represent at once the sacred and the profane, the general and the specific, the intrinsic and the extrinsic, the perpetual and the frail, the Hellenic and the Hebraic. In fact I think it is the responsibility of architects to attempt to represent both sides of the coin, without synthesis. The given present and an inevitable future can be served simultaneously, without nullifying either.

Synthesis has, more than any other single factor, mystified the practice of architecture and encouraged imprecise thinking. It has vitiated the study of the opposing conditions that are present in each and every building and project. Whereas law and medicine engage in precision and succinctness, architecture masks these qualities, avoiding demystification—all while extolling the general values of transformation and synthesis.

In following the development of my work from synthesis toward thesis/antithesis, I hope to show the potential architecture has for a powerful mode of expression in the simultaneous statement of opposing values.

VERSUS: An American Architect's Alternatives

An irreverent review of the nine lives (chapters) of an anti-Platonic architectural career that reflects the kaleidoscopic period in America from 1960 to 1980, mirroring more than one hundred projects steeped in the fashion(s) of the times. Beginning within the tradition of synthesis, the attitudes and the buildings herein shift socially and stylistically, moving ultimately toward a position of talmudic reasoning that simultaneously explicates the two sides of an emerging, albeit controversial, architectural argument.

One: Mies van der Rohe-Influenced, Chicago-School Contextual Phase 1953–1981

Mies van der Rohe's influence on me was the first in a series that succeeded in forcing me to see things with a certain bias in the context of a preexisting synthetic architectural language. It lasted for more than a quarter of a century, and began in the 1950s in Chicago when that city was at the peak of its Miesian heyday. I was a designer in the Chicago office of Skidmore, Owings and Merrill and because I was eager to adopt the currency of the times in order to be accepted since I had no architectural credentials (I had flunked out of the Massachusetts Institute of Technology in 1949), I jumped aboard the van der Rohe bandwagon there. Owing to the fact that I had not been actually schooled in the structuralist/formalist dogma of the Miesian Illinois Institute of Technology, my early projects in this idiom are stiltedly awkward. Later projects like Boardwalk and Loop College are direct rip-offs of the first Mies high-rise apartment building constructed at Lafayette Park in Detroit, Michigan, and, as such, develop the codified vernacular not at all. My interest in tall buildings, as Miesian efforts, continued until the end of the 1970s and manifested itself in ironic comments on the idiom such as, for example, Pensacola II. Other architects worked in the Mies manner more successfully than I and they include almost anyone who attended IIT and/or was committed to the discipline. But the Mies influence was so pervasive in Chicago for that twenty-five year span that even architects like myself, who were neither trained nor particularly motivated to work in that métier, did so in the end anyway.

Conceptual Atrium House
Project, 1953

Drawn by Robert Claiborne

Largely based on my early interpretations of Mies van der Rohe, this conceptual piece was also influenced by Philip Johnson's atrium project for John D. Rockefeller 3rd in Manhattan. Note how the street-facing wall is just high enough to conceal whatever is beyond it, and so masks the function of the building.

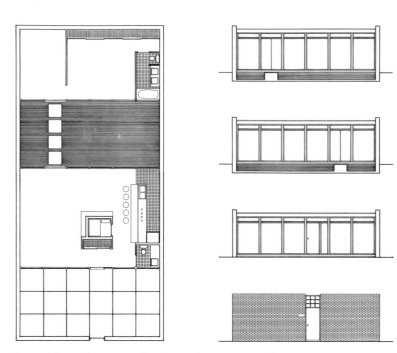

Ground floor plan, street elevation and transverse sections

In looking back I believe I first became aware of Mies van der Rohe's influence on the way I thought about architecture when I was in the U.S. Navy. Before I enlisted in 1950—and while I was in a so-called architectural partnership (I had previously spent a year apprenticing for George Fred and William Keck)—I had met Herbert Greenwald, the developer of many apartment building complexes designed by Mies (the association between the two men has been thoroughly documented and along with Henry Heald, then president of IIT, Greenwald was the closest thing to a patron of Mies). I don't really know why Greenwald took a liking to me, but he did, and we began to correspond while I was in the Navy. Whether it was that he had been a rabbinical student or had a genuine vision about housing, Greenwald managed to convey a powerful sense of zealotry—purpose of mission if you will—that I later came to identify with Mies. I'm not sure how much of this zeal of Greenwald's was the product of my own overworked imagination—or of my thrill at befriending someone as important as Greenwald—but for whatever conceits I was influenced to write down my thoughts about architecture. In connection with these meanderings on paper, I designed my first Miesian project in 1953.

A little urban infill house tucked between two neighbors and reminiscent of Philip Johnson's 1950 Rockefeller Guest House in New York City, it was my first attempt at "designing." Its design reflects, however, more my beginning interests in the Modernism of Mies's emerging Chicago style than Johnson's Guest House. At the time I identified with Chicago and wanted desperately to "come home" to work within the context of the legitimacy of the times, and the times (I perceived) were clearly entering an age of Miesian-influenced architecture. This first little Mies project also shows the influence of Mies's 1930s German court houses.

Mies van der Rohe's influence on me did not become enduring, however, until I began work as a designer in the Chicago office of Skidmore, Owings and Merrill in 1957. Although I worked there on the U.S. Air Force Academy (not a particularly hard-core Miesian project), I found that many of the people in the design department with me had been trained by Mies at the Illinois Institute of Technology.

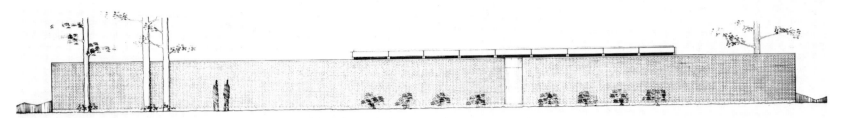

Street elevation and transverse sections

Atrium House Project, Evanston, Illinois, 1958

This was my first project for an actual client, albeit unbuilt. The Italian critic Manfredo Tafuri's Deathly Mask of Silence (the street wall) is lowered barely enough to reveal the flat roof beyond. No more of a revelation than that, still it is a move toward an expressive act. Preceded by Philip Johnson's (1942) Cambridge house designed for his own use and postdated by Anderson Todd's Houston Atrium House (1964), this design confirms the Miesian message in the air.

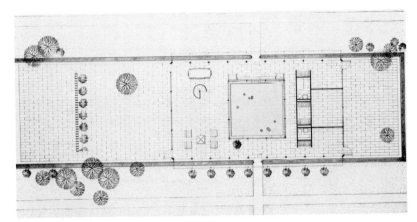

Ground floor plan

This second-hand Miesian influence first showed itself in my work in a brace of steel furniture I designed for my own apartment. Influenced by Knoll Associates' recently produced residential line (which in turn had been influenced by Mies's cruciform four-angle column for the German Pavilion at Barcelona of 1929), the furniture was suitable for—and eclectically timely in—the Chicago of the late 1950s. Two other architects and I also attempted to convince U.S. Steel either to extrude or roll a cruciform steel column reminiscent of the one at the German Pavilion. Being at SOM in the late 1950s often led to retrograde studies like that.

My next application of the cruciform column (by now my obsession) was in the design of a Miesian urban court house in 1958 for my first actual client. (I had begun to moonlight while at SOM as did many of my friends there.) The atrium house was very popular at that time (for example, José Luis Sert's own house in Cambridge, Massachusetts, and projects by Howard Barnstone and Anderson Todd in Houston, Texas) and a spate of sycophantic books on Mies began to be published by Peter Blake, Ludwig Hilberseimer, Arthur Drexler, Werner Blaser, ad nauseam. My interest in this project revolved around the constructional possibilities in the application of the cruciform column and not in any formal motives. I had no intention of evoking any new emotional responses, and even hid the Miesian structural clarity of this project behind the dumb wall separating the public from whatever presumably wonderful events went on behind the blank facade. Clearly European in origin, the "secured" introversion of this house was as opportune in the work of Miesians in Chicago of the 1950s as it was in that of Rationalists in the Swiss canton of Ticino of the late 1970s.

In 1959 I left Chicago for New Haven, Yale and Paul Rudolph and the next time Miesianism appears in my work is in my master's thesis project of 1961. Since I did not feel sufficiently secure with the new Brutalist language Paul Rudolph was training us all to speak, I reverted to type in this project. The scheme was based on an actual project then under study by SOM for the new University of Illinois, Chicago Circle Campus and being master-planned on a variety of sites. Since I was officially on leave from SOM (I actu-

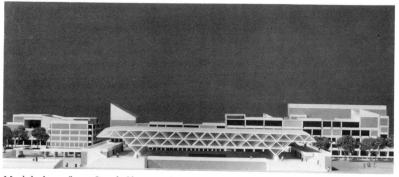

Model photo from South Shore Drive looking east

**Master's Thesis Project,
Yale University, 1961**

My final project under Paul
Rudolph's direction at Yale shows
little of the influence of Rudolphian "push-pull, click-click" architecture (the agitated surface
treatment of Rudolph's buildings

in which facades advance to, and
recede from, the picture plane).
The structural frame and compositional campus planning all vainly
conspire to Miesian contextualism, while the empty body of
water at the center discourages
any potential activity the campus
might otherwise have provided.

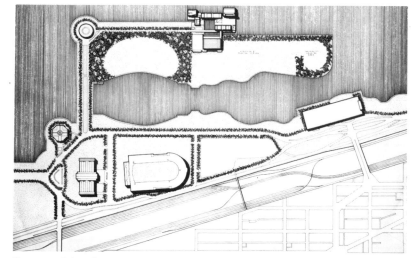

Contextual site plan

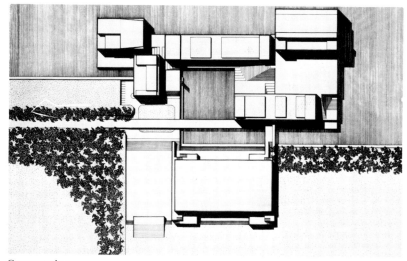

Campus plan

ally did go back for a short time after graduating), I had
access to planning and programming information dealing
with this project at SOM. In its use of compositional campus-planning techniques and containment of functions
within a structural frame, the project owes a debt to the Miesian Chicago to which I was about to return. Reverting to type
was certainly no guarantee of success at Rudolphian Yale and
my master's thesis was without doubt not my most successful
project at Yale. My interest in Mies's frame—in his defined
scope of architecture—was to rise up again and again
throughout the next twenty years. But before letting it take
form, I synthesized it in words.

   After I returned to Chicago and had been almost two years
in partnership with an architect with whom I had worked at
SOM, Norman Koglin, I began teaching at the University of
Illinois in Chicago in 1963. This led me to try to put into
words the architectural commitments I felt at the time and to
deal with the poetry I sensed was implicit in the Mies argu-

Perspective drawing looking east

Apartment Building Project,
Boca Raton, Florida, 1972

Assisted by John Haley

A cross-wall configuration in which the structure and repeated modulation imply a congruity of purpose, this project owes as much to Modernist planning principles as it does to Mies. His taut functional plan-configurations and an interior street try to pretend the surrounding alien sea of parking doesn't exist. Supporting the developer's pragmatism, the design demonstrates how far Mies's influence has fallen from formal Utopian grace into an "end-justifies-the-means" mentality.

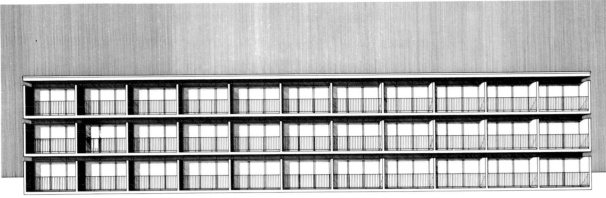

Typical (north and south) elevation

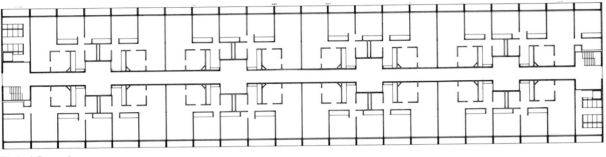

Typical floor plans

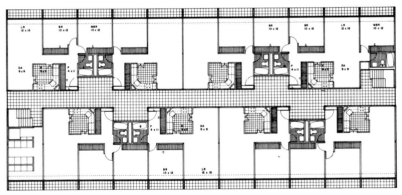

Typical floor plans

ment. Two years later I expanded on this thesis by writing a paper that attempted polemically to justify even further my newfound Mies position. I was determined to verbalize a synthetic attitude toward Chicago that I deemed appropriate for the times. The ideas in this paper, *Toward the Completion of a Cycle*,[1] were not to find fruition in my work until the 1960s were over, however, for I became involved with two other concerns of the moment: megastructures and egalitarianism. It wasn't until 1972, in another series of projects, that I looked again to Mies for inspiration.

The first of these projects was a cross-wall three-story residential project in Boca Raton, Florida, interestingly for Herbert Greenwald's son, Bennet Greenwald, who, like his father, had become a real estate developer. Fortunately the project never got built. For all its correct orientation, brissoleil rationality and general background quality—indicating a presumably mature way of dealing with housing problems—the sea of parking and generally inhumane ap-

Office Building Project,
Chicago, 1972

My only attempt at cladding the frame, this unbuilt project curtsies in the general direction of Mies's IBM, Seagram and Illinois Center without either significantly improving the genre or even dealing, as the Master himself did, with large- and small-scale proportional problems. Actually a diagram, it is characteristic of how many architects (significantly SOM) used Miesian methods simplistically to convey programmatic resolutions within what for all the world looked like "architecture."

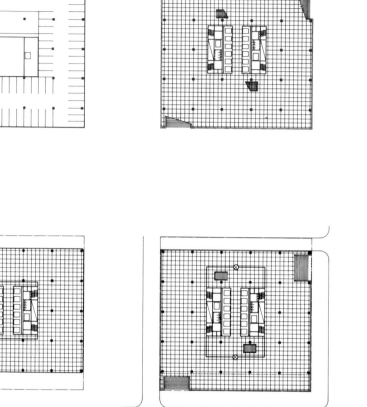
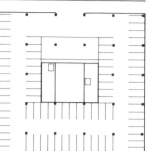

Plaza, parking, typical floor plans and typical elevation

proach of the project vitiate any redeeming responsible features it might have had. Nonetheless I was determined to build in the Mies métier, but before I did, I worked on another unbuilt project for Bennet Greenwald.

A classical program for a very Chicago-like unclassical problem (speculative office blocks), this office building project was more pragmatic than adventurous (but by 1972 many of the speculative office buildings of Mies's descendant firm were also). The classical odd-bay scheme of earlier Mies is here replaced by a clumsy four-by-five bay tower, the height of which was determined by zoning and economics more than by formal concerns. At ground level the dumb wall of my 1953 court house now acts as the plinth. The structure, which is clad, looks more toward later Mies (Commonwealth Promenade Apartments, Esplanade Apartments, Lafayette Park Apartments, Seagram) than to

the structural expressionism of his earlier American work. It portrays unabashed eclecticism, without the necessity for being grammatically correct, moving toward a new, economically motivated synthesis.

The Mies box I finally built in 1971–74, however, did look back to the expression of the frame—the same one I think I was alluding to almost ten years earlier when I wrote *Toward the Completion of a Cycle.* A straight-line descendant of the Mies building at Lafayette Park in Detroit, Boardwalk's primary facades are expansions of each square unitary glazed opening. Golden-sectionized, the building interprets Chicago's grid plan, which is contextualized as a matrix. It is mature, responsible and just a little bit boring. Careful in its quoting of early Mies, it is strangely heedless of piloted canonical Mies at its ground plane where it denies the pedestrian any visual access. Nonetheless Boardwalk (the project

Boardwalk Apartment Building, Chicago, Illinois, 1971–74

Assisted by John Haley, Ralph Johnson, Bruce Thurman
Structural engineer: Cohen, Barretto, Marchertas
Mechanical and electrical engineer: Wallace & Migdal
Photography: Ruyell Ho and Philip Turner

My first (and only) built project inspired by Mies van der Rohe looks to his first built high-rise at Lafayette Park (Detroit) and to the early infill methods of his Promontory Apartments and 860 Lake Shore Drive rather than to his later more sophisticated skinning techniques, which were ultimately so influential on the American tall building. With both the superstructure and the individual framed openings organized as a kind of homage to the square and the solar bronze glass and duranodic sash golden-sectionized, the whole is thought contextually to be a study in Chicago good taste.

Elevation perspective drawing from west

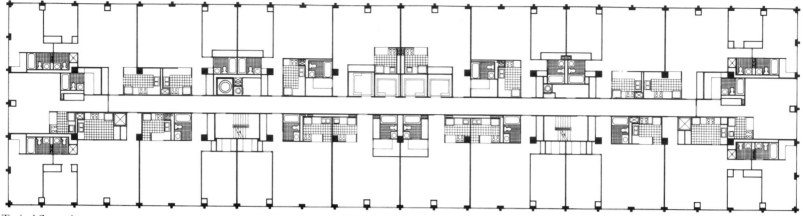

Typical floor plan

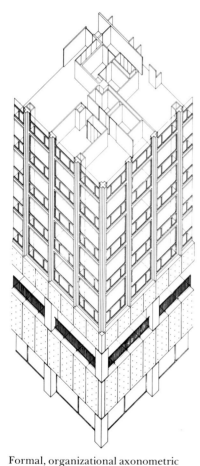

Formal, organizational axonometric

Entrance canopy and facade

Model apartment—living/dining room

was one of several for the same developer: Park Place, Reading Railroad, Marvin Gardens, etc.) is at home in Chicago where so many other Mies rip-offs quietly coexist with the Master's work. In fact, given half a chance I might have done several more of the same basic building. After all when Mies died in August, 1969, all of us in Chicago chanted "le roi est mort" and all the best new Chicago buildings seemed to cry "vive le roi."

The reuse of the Boardwalk motif logically came in the first series of designs for the next project I did for the same client, Pensacola I. Luckily this project didn't really get under way for another seven years by which time the project (and I) would have undergone serious changes. But I did do another self-quoting exercise in the mid-1970s, Loop College, ironi-

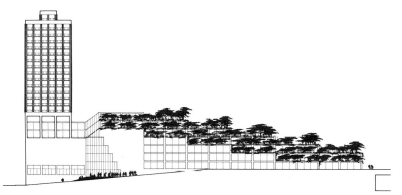

West elevation

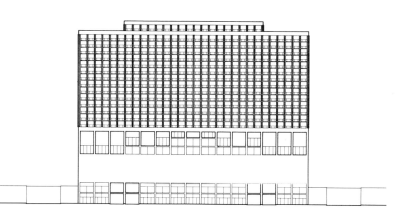

North elevation

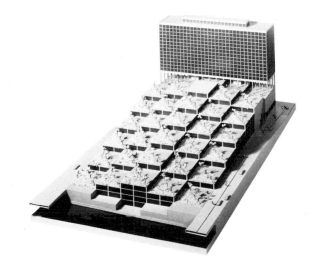

Model view from west

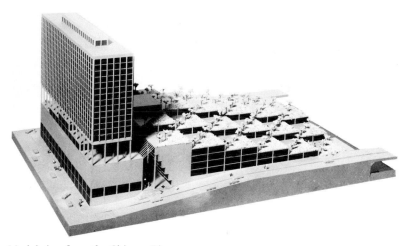

Model view from the Chicago River

Loop College Project,
Chicago, 1974

Assisted by John Haley

As in all my earlier tower schemes, this project for an unbuilt downtown junior college rises Utopianlike from a "profane" base of urbanity toward a Platonic idealism. With its superstructure typically lifted above the urban variegated functions by pilotis, Loop College is Ville-Radieuse van der Rohe on the Chicago River.

cally in competition with Mies's descendant firm (we both lost). Pensacola I and Loop College have bases far more agitated (or activated, depending on your point of view) than has Pensacola II—the project that was actually built. The towers for Loop College and Pensacola I are still by the book.

By the time of Pensacola II, I had a sufficient sense of self, combined with a growing comprehension of the case for dualistic thought, to deal with it in ways I would never have dreamed possible when designing Boardwalk. In the first place the program itself was fascinating. The client wished the new building to duplicate the nearby existing Boardwalk building, creating thereby an image of parallel apartment towers when viewed from Lake Shore Drive. But the program also included a large commercial shopping mall and

Pensacola Place II Apartment
Project, Chicago, 1978–81

Associate-in-charge:
Robert Fugman
Assisted by Philip Holden,
Thomas Horan, Robert
Caddigan, Polly Hawkins
Structural engineer: Cohen,
Barretto, Marchertas
Mechanical and electrical
engineer: Wallace & Migdal

The Janus piece to Boardwalk,
this middle-income housing and
commercial complex struggles
with its schizophrenic site. On one
side are Lake Shore Drive and the
wealthy; on the other the ghosts of
Mies and Sullivan, symbolically on
axis in Graceland Cemetery, and
the working class passing by in
public transportation. Thus
imbalanced the complex denies
resolution, the difference between
the two facades becoming even
more pronounced when they are
juxtaposed.

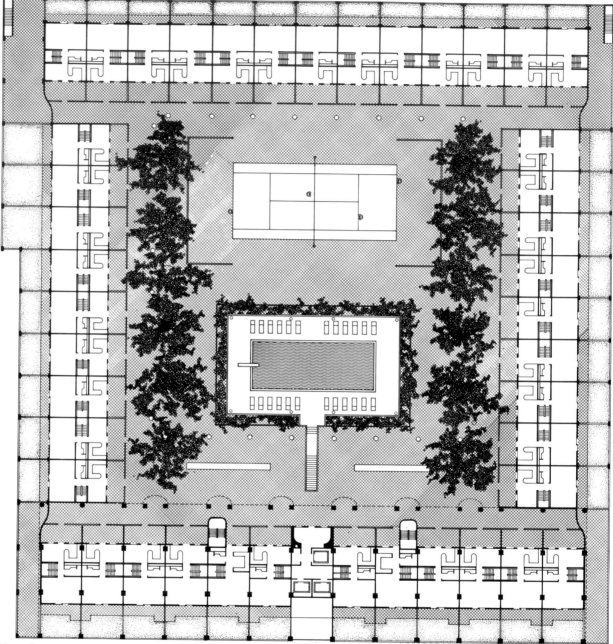

Plaza plan

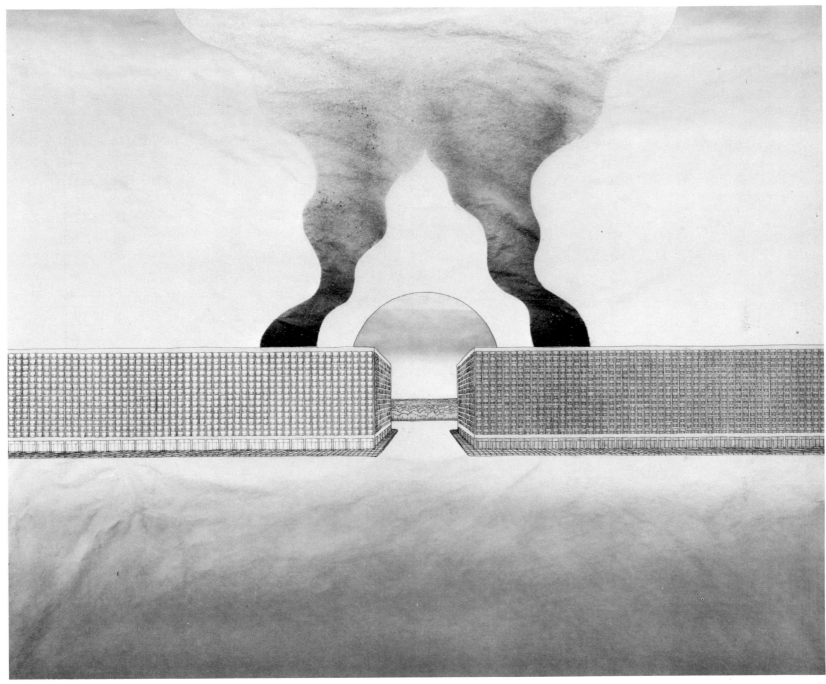

Conceptual extension as linear city

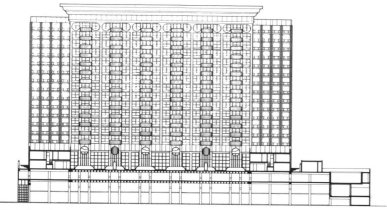

West elevation/section

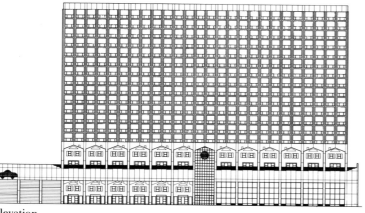

East elevation

View of commercial mall

numerous town houses on a plaza deck that would be blocked from view from the drive by a series of existing four-story buildings. Any specific iconic imagery explaining the town houses and commercial shopping mall, therefore, would be seen only if purposely looked for on approaching the complex. When the decision was made to describe the iconic house and archetypal commercial facade typologically (the primary entrance to the complex would be a narthex to real estate development replete with rose window as exhaust grille), it was all done *sotto voce* since none of it would make its presence felt except on deliberate examination.

The east facade is thus thought of as having the typologies of the city imprinted on it: commercial building, town house and, finally, the alienating grid of office/apartment tower. The west facade is something else again. Here the "tasteful" bronze-tinted glass and golden-sectioned duranodic sash of the east facade are replaced by a giant order consisting of balconies as pilasters holding up ionic cutouts—all supporting an entablature concealing rooftop mechanical equipment. Windows infilling this giant order are made of black-tinted glass with black-anodized mullions; they face the ghosts of Sullivan and Mies in Graceland Cemetery.

A conceptual piece on this complex, entitled *Optimism and Skepticism and the Linear City*,[2] describes Chicago as a linear city and also contends with the Modern movement in architecture.

The last of the projects in this phase is not an architectural project per se. It is a photo-collage called The Titanic, copies of which I mailed to all the orthodoxy I could think of offering to sell them one-way tickets for a ride on The Titanic. Assembled in 1978 along with a *Letter to Mies*,[3] it is more a reflection of the end of the 1970s than of any momentous occasion such as for example the end of a certain phase of my own work. Really determined sycophants nonetheless may see it as Crown Hall rising from the depths just as iconoclasts may see it as the watershed structure sinking. Given embattled Chicago it could also as easily be seen as Crown Hall simply—if tenuously—afloat.

These twenty-five years and twelve projects were part of a phase I never really felt was mine—a phase that was more like lifting weights in preparation for climbing into the ring than anything else. It was a naive and reassuring phase in which I saw Chicago as a city, according to Nory Miller in her

The Titanic, 1978, Photo-collage

essay in the catalogue *American Architectural Alternatives,* under "German [Miesian] occupation."

The work that falls within this phase was the result of a deteriorating Platonic frame of mind. Generally the projects owed their existence, through Mies, to traditional Hellenic ideals but individually they were eroded by the vast shift that was occurring in architecture and in American politics in the 1960s and 1970s, in the course of which simplistic thought was radically transformed. In architecture the messages sent out in the late 1960s by Robert Venturi corresponded with the political transformation. In fact, what Viet Nam was to America, I would contend, Venturi was to architecture. Each dealt a terminal blow to simplistic thought and caused the fall from grace of a particular group and each was early, and heavily, criticized for forcing the realization on America that patriotism and the Zeitgeist theory were passé. Viet Nam and Venturi are owed a great debt for bringing poignancy into American life and American architecture, and for focusing national concern on the country's cultural roots. America and architecture came to maturity during this time and with this maturity came the major struggle with dualistic thought that forms an important part of Post-Modernism. I have come to identify this dualism, which can be seen in this phase of my work, with talmudic thought—that is, the concept of the simultaneous study of opposites without the necessity of creating a new synthesis.

The Pensacola II project best illustrates my own position. Here the two parallel facades of the primary tower stand in opposition to, and take strength from, one another. This attitude is very different from that expressed by Mies in 1924 in his paper *Baukunst und Zeitwille:* "We are concerned today with questions of a general nature. The individual is losing significance; his destiny is no longer what interests us. The decisive achievements in all fields are impersonal and their authors are for the most part unknown. They are part of the trend of our time towards anonymity." In Platonic philosophy all things are measured against a divine condition and this was obviously at the root of Mies's *tabula rasa* position. But by the late 1960s (indeed, at the end of Mies's life) this attitude no longer seemed the only way for architecture to evolve. The ability to sense both the perpetual and the finite condition in architecture started to emerge when schismatic Modernism came under fire. In my case, it took about a decade longer than most architects, partly because of my slow-motion conceptual shifting, with Pensacola II finally being the result.

1. *Toward the Completion of a Cycle,* 1965

In architecture, the Industrial Revolution secured for Chicago an historic foothold; it took form in an expression of a skeleton frame as both structure and space, a matrix. It was inevitable that an essential, simple organization of space through structure occur in Chicago, in that here was a city that had no excessive layers of sophistry in apriori culture manifest in form. It was inevitable because of the appropriateness of the city's orthogonal grid and single-minded linearity to accept another kind of grid flung into space. It was inevitable because the revolution was clearly an American one and this was the only clear American city. That structural, spatial, skeleton frame came to be the generator of the Chicago School and was the first modulated matrix. It was, and still is, the most powerful example of that which is implicit in the combination of structure and space. It was, and still is, the best example of the field theory of architecture over and against the compositional theory of architecture. It was, and still is, the most logical extension known of two dimension implying, and then becoming, three dimension.

The beginning of this century saw Frank Lloyd Wright extend knowledge of structure combined with space into the compositional theory of dynamic symmetry placed on the same two-dimensional grid of Chicago. The implications of this juxtaposition were many, and curiously, were to bear fruit not in Chicago but in Europe. Through the exhibiting of Wright's work early in the century the young architects of Europe, who were then trying to break with the neoclassic traditions then rampant, were fascinated with the Wrightian juxtapositions and the influence was clearly felt in De Stijl, the Bauhaus, and Constructivism. They were most clearly felt in the young Mies van der Rohe. He was to demonstrate this influence from the brick villa of 1923 through the court houses of the thirties. There was, however, a synthesis of the Wrightian juxtaposition of freely composed space defining structure with the two-dimensional grid of the midwestern city. Mies's juxtaposition was more closely related in that the planar definers of space tended to be nonstructural and were disposed to a field grid of point structure. In 1938 Mies inevitably comes to Chicago. In field as point structure, which in Germany was the counterpoint now in the field as city was to become Mies's raison d'être. The American technology of steel which had lain dormant in Mies's hands since the inception of the Chicago School was to find ultimate expression of slenderness and tension. The spatial thesis of Wright, however, as well as that of the early Mies was subjugated. The tilting up into space of the Chicago grid did not become a three-dimensional matrix with Mies, but rather a juxtaposition of two-dimensional planes, the two-dimensionality of which was made more clear by the articulation of the corners. The resulting forms were an enveloping rather than an extending of space through structure.

Inevitably there was a powerful rejection of this concept by the very descendants of the eastern eclectics Louis Sullivan had once described. Their rejection, as all reactions to ideas just preceding, was to totally ignore any and all of that which had been most recently accomplished, and to rather draw as formal generators notions from history further removed from their contemporary epoch.

This has forced an extremely chaotic result. It is not so bad to be an eclectic, if by that one means the logical extension of pragmatic ideas developed in sequence by man. So it is in our time that the acknowledgment of those rational forces in sequence giving form to our technological epoch makes sense.

And so the return to the rational mainstream of twentieth century technology in combination with man's desire to mold space finds its life blood in the very matrix that was originally implied by the three-dimensional possibilities of the structural frame, not as envelope but as the meshing of interior and exterior space in the ordered context of structure. In the framework of rational thought, this might then be the synthesis of all those forces which have brought us to this moment in time.

These forces do not necessarily make art. Discipline does not necessarily make art. There is no art without discipline.

Art can be construed to be the arbitrariness of the sensibilities. Art can be construed to deal with the sophistries of man.

I leave you to art, and if a preference must be made, mine would be in favor of rational thought. Art may come.

2. *Optimism and Skepticism and the Linear City,* 1979

Modern life was, by its very nature, optimistic. The revolution secured for all a new beginning. Futurists, Dadaists, Suprematists alike all pointed to a Utopian life where industrialized egalitarianism would, once and for all, dispose of an unnecessary aristocracy and its archeological residue—architecture. The first two decades of modern life were dramatized by the polemical journalese of both magazines *l'Architecture vivante* and *l'Art nouveau.* Unfortunately the third decade produced an international depression, while the fourth decade produced another major holocaust. It wasn't until the fifth and sixth decades of modern life that the early polemical pursuits were realized, and by then the need for fulfillment was so great that the original pure optimism was buried by an epoch that gorged itself on the concretization of an intellectual concept. Fifty years had transpired, life was still pure and not much had really changed.

Now the fifty years before that (you know, the one Louis Sullivan had belatedly decried) had been filled with the icons of *its* own origins. It had roots and ties and all sorts of connective tissue grafted onto its own evolution. Unfortunately, it had something else as well. It represented the vestigial link with the Black Prince, the omnipotent Church and the all-powerful State, and, as such, became the Auschwitz of the Aristocracy. The very mention of "The Orders" or ornament brought about Loosian hysteria and Beaux Arts training was considered retardataire and evoked skepticism. It was thus that nineteenth-century humanism was dissipated and replaced by twentieth-century intellectualism and the city of man came into conflict with man's ideas about his city.

Now the linear city has two sides, as in its life lies its death—not life after death, for that is a concept—but rather life and death such as the two sides of a coin whose future and whose past are mirrored in its faces but whose presence is represented by its thin present. The linear city is in eternal conflict. Its schizophrenia is represented by a Utopian optimism mirroring a desired future opposing the ultimate skepticism—knowledge of the finite condition of Man.

3. *Letter to Mies,* 1978

Dear Mies:

I miss you. I wish you were here to see what's happened. The state of architecture has grown curiouser and curiouser in the ten years you've been gone. There's something called "Post-Modernism" now that seems to be getting everyone's attention. I guess it means to be something more than just "after modern architecture," which is not to suggest that there aren't even those who think modern architecture failed. Can you believe there are even mutterings about the death of modern architecture? But don't worry—it's very much alive. People are doing something called "high-tech" now, which I guess is supposed to deal with industrialization one more time. There's a guy in California called Helmut Schultz who even did a house with all exposed structure and right here in Chicago there's someone called Helmut Jahn who does the same thing only at a much larger scale. They're both German, of course, and Jahn has even been called "Baron von High Tech."

Here in Chicago everything appears to have remained much the same as it was ten years ago. The axis you left behind to run your firm seems to be thriving and the rest of your descendancy is alive and well and at work (at least in Chicago). Your followers at SOM are totally victorious now that Walter Netsch is taking early retirement but I think it has taken a big toll in their health.

You'll be interested to know that lots of "Mies Buildings" are now being designed for Arabs though there seems to be some small concern in this country about "four-square" buildings with too much glass—something about energy conservation.

The Illinois Institute of Technology is the same as it was ten years ago. The architecture school is still the same old Jesuit Seminary it was when you were here and they still import seminarians from the Black Forest for graduate school who still believe in your credo: "Build, don't talk." You really had Chicago figured out when you said that all the New York intellectuals mostly talk to each other anyway. For a while there was cause for alarm when Jim Freed was Dean. He went around hiring people who didn't graduate from IIT, brought in a lot of weird New York types as lecturers and even tried to change the curriculum. I couldn't believe it—he actually thought color had something to do with architecture. Not to worry though—they ran him out of town and things are back to what they were before you left.

Some things do worry me about Chicago, though. When you were here the C. F. Murphy firm was solid with first Jacques Brownson and then Gener Sommers in control. Now, this fellow Helmut Jahn is doing some strange things. I've heard he even has a pediment on one of his buildings. There's even an architect who teaches at IIT named Tom Beeby who had designed one project that looks like the Parthenon and another one with Minarets. Luck-

ily they're not being built, but it's worrisome all the same. Imagine, they even gave him tenure at IIT. Then, there's this crazy group called the "Chicago Seven" that goes around stirring up trouble by talking a lot instead of building. They have architecture shows in galleries, produce catalogs, hold seminars, conduct competitions and are generally rather bothersome. Worst of all, they seem to be incredulously irreverent when it comes to your followers. Can you imagine—they're even redoing the Chicago Tribune competition of 1922 as a drawing show at the Museum of Contemporary Art!

Incidentally, you were right about Philip Johnson. Those damn intellectuals are all the same. He's done a high-rise in New York City right out of Boullée and Chippendale and now he's doing another one in Pittsburgh that's Houses-of-Parliament Gothic. I can't believe what an influence he is still having with young architects. Then there's Robert Venturi. Three years before you left he wrote this awful little book about complexity or something and now everybody seems to have read it and the buildings he is doing are plainly crazy. He's even doing a nightclub with classical columns. Just before you left there was that new Dean at Yale—Charles Moore—and he's even done a piazza in New Orleans with his own face on a wall spouting water. They're all the same. That's why I really like Chicago—buildings really mean something here—you can touch them, you can rent them, they're made out of something, there's not all that funny so-called idea content to contend with. Sullivan and Giedion and Pevsner were right after all.

That's about it, I guess. Oh, as far as me…well, you always thought I was kind of silly. At least that much hasn't changed. I do miss you though.

Love,
Stanley

Two: De Stijlian, Rudolphian, Brutalist Phase 1960–1967

The work in this category—my De Stijlian, Rudolphian, Brutalist phase—was influenced at first by the painter Mondrian, in whom I had developed an interest when I started to paint while I was in the U.S. Navy. From an interest in Mondrian, who was an early member of the De Stijl group, it was but a short jump to becoming fascinated with the architectural members of that group. My connections with architectural and painterly antecedents were intensified when I came under the pervasive influence of both the architect Paul Rudolph and the painter Josef Albers at Yale's art and architecture schools. The times (the early to mid-1960s) also saw the waning of high-Mies Modernism and many architects, like me, were casting about and trying on new clothes. Many of my projects have a sense of materiality (almost all are conceived in brick—built or unbuilt) and are heavy, direct and unsophisticated. Very few of them have a quality of wholeness; mostly they break up as though in a conceptual seismic shift. Architects who functioned much better than I did in this métier were Ulrich Franzen, Paul Rudolph (of course), John Johansen, Edward Larrabee Barnes and, to some extent, Harry Weese. They were all somewhat influenced by the neo-Brutalism of Le Corbusier, perhaps best manifested in his Maisons Jaoul in France, and by the early James Stirling, who was perhaps the most successful in incorporating Le Corbusier stylistic moves into his early work. But Paul Rudolph was the architect who had the biggest influence on my work at the time, primarily because I was both his student and his employee while at Yale and because our friendship lasted for many years after I left Yale.

Paul Rudolph's influence steered me away from my Germanic Chicagoese 1950s style and pinpointed the new Brutalist direction my work was to take. Since I had always been interested in the neoplasticism of Mondrian and the fragmented cubism of the De Stijl architects, it was a natural direction for me. Rudolph's influence came even more naturally in terms of my involvement with Mies. Although Mies's and Rudolph's buildings appear to vary widely many of their underlying formal concepts are similar. Both their buildings, for example, are couched in the reductive syntax of Modernism and are thus inward looking; they are not socially responsive nor do they communicate to a large public through familiar symbols. Suffice it to say that the transition from one brand of hermeticism to another was easy.

It would be too simplistic, however, merely to lump Mies's Platonism with Rudolph's Brutalism inasmuch as the former contains Zeitgeist propositions for our time while the latter rebels against the very concept of any spirit of the age. The struggle between these two concepts would be apparent in my work for two decades. My dissatisfaction with perfection—no doubt borne out of wedlock since my knowledge of the Miesian spirit was by no means comprehensive at the time and I was not necessarily convinced of its lasting values—was symbolized in at least a part of my work by a lack of resolution. Luckily I was too young to indulge in the zealous rhetoric of Miesian mysticism while the Yale/Rudolphian modality seemed to offer me greater possibilities for staking out my own territory. What I ended up doing was to replace one Modernist revolutionary hero with another—Le Corbusier for Mies van der Rohe. Formal manipulation became the new game and its rules were different from those of Chicago's reductive structural thought.

The first project that cut structural Chicago's taut umbilical cord was my bachelor's thesis at Yale in 1960, with Paul Rudolph as my thesis critic. An apartment project tower located on the near South Side in Chicago, it is at once asymmetrical (a pinwheel) and monolithic (a nine-square set piece). Its structure is nonetheless obscure and its scale is shifted (the split-level helps) so that the tower sits uneasily upon its base. Obviously influenced by Rudolph's criticism the project was more the rule than the exception in the late 1950s and early 1960s at Yale (see Robert A. M. Stern, "Yale 1950–1965," *Oppositions 4:* 35-62). While it predates Moshe Safdie's Habitat it postdates the many projects at Yale equally influenced by Rudolph's not-so-subtle hand. But I was there for his influence and if my student work looks as though the Master's hand had been upon it that was how a lot of work produced at Yale looked in those years: like voluntary exercises in the Rudolphian architectural look-alike drill team.

By 1960 Paul Rudolph's architectural drawings and his built work were sufficiently published to pose an influence well beyond Yale, and I continued working in his métier through at least a part of the master's program with Rudolph as studio critic. The Yale Science Library Project of 1960 and the Blue Cross-Blue Shield Office Building Project of 1961 strongly reflect my continuing development along Rudolphian stylistic lines, while not demonstrating any particular grasp of the underlying reasons for working in that idiom. Yale during that time was anything but semiologically engaged—Rudolph had imbued the student body with the fervency of formal manipulation without either the social posturing that came later under Charles Moore's stewardship at Yale or the comprehensive (if ironic) historicism of Robert Venturi. Certainly there was nothing in my background to suggest such concerns.

On returning to Chicago in June, 1961—and after the briefest possible time fulfilling my obligations to SOM—I accepted a position with Harry Weese, which he described as his Chief of Design. Within six months I left Weese and formed a partnership with Norman Koglin. Needless to say the work of that partnership—and for many years that of my own independent practice—reflected Rudolph's influence. In the 1960s architects measured their position against his muscle-flexing, push-pull, click-click architecture. Rudolph was at the apogee of his career.

All of this is by way of saying that I was seeking some brand of credibility. I had always felt that architecture had a vitally legitimate center and I was determined to be at that center, intellectually speaking. By the beginning of the 1960s Rudolph seemed to many of us to personify that center in his practice and in his teaching. By the time I established my

Boardwalk Apartment Building, Chicago, Illinois, 1971–74. View of tower superstructure from west

Pensacola Place II Apartment Project, Chicago, Illinois, 1978–81. Rendering of entire project looking toward Boardwalk

Pensacola Place II. Rendering of plaza deck featuring base of tower and plaza town houses (looking north)

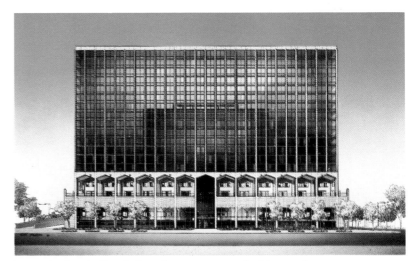

Pensacola Place II. Rendering of tower entrance (looking west)

Pickwick Village, 1963–64. View from west

Stacked Maisonette Project, 1964. Rendering of project from northwest

Urban Matrix, Chicago, Illinois, 1967–68. Brobidignan Venetian canal and causeway

Instant City, 1965–66. Aerial view of two models

Site plan

Bachelor's Thesis Project,
Yale University, New Haven,
Connecticut, 1960

This project represents my first real break with Chicago and Mies. The tall-building skeleton frame is replaced by a crosswall made of prefabricated concrete structural elements that reflect and define the spaces and also make up the primary formal generator. A study in Modernist asymmetric concerns of the day, it finds justification in its mathematical, pinwheel origin (during the late 1950s Walter Netsch and Bertrand Goldberg, as well as Paul Rudolph, were embroiled in geometry as a panacea). The ultimate, irrational extension of Henri Sauvage—for everyone a (leaking) terrace—it was actually concretized in a not entirely different form in Laprairie Basin, Quebec, by Moshe Safdie in 1967.

Photograph of model (sculpture by Robert Engman)

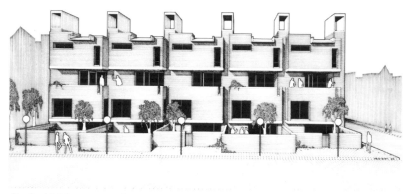

Stacked Maisonette project streetscape

Pickwick Plaza street elevation

Pickwick Village (1963–64), Pickwick Plaza (1963) and Stacked Maisonette Project (1964)

In association with Norman A. Koglin
Assisted by Stuart Beatty and Laurence Booth
Photography: Philip Turner

These three De Stijlian/Rudolphian-influenced housing projects while somewhat contextually influenced are clearly based on Le Corbusier's Maisons Jaoul. Individual unitization may have seemed admirable at the time but here it overwhelms any notion of overall group identification to such an extent that (at least in Pickwick Village and the Stacked Maisonette project) the units look as though, given half a chance, they would smartly march, one after the other, down the block.

Pickwick Village view from northwest

Car porch

Habenicht House, Nottingham
Woods, Elburn, Illinois, 1962–63

In association with
Norman A. Koglin
Photography: Philip Turner

Brazenly reminiscent of Rudolphian Yale, the house is neither free-plan Modern nor traditionally holistic in its androgynous interlocking and interpenetration of itself. Thus agitated it represents yearning combined with frustration, all bereft of either position or polemic.

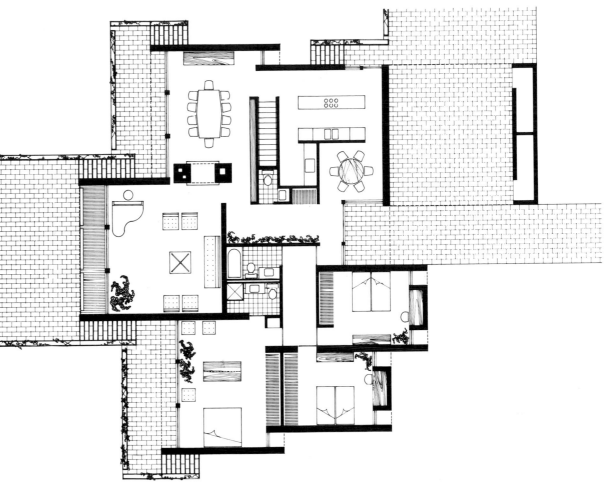
Ground floor plan

partnership with Koglin, I felt I had just the ticket to design my way into contemporaneity.

During the course of the next eight years (two of which were spent in partnership with Koglin) eight buildings were built that reflected my continuing interest in the De Stijlian philosophy. Contextualism is minimally evident in the fact that many of the projects are fragmented sufficiently to bely any notion of wholeness and—in the case of the Pickwick Village town house project at least—that they have individual rhythmic qualities to set them in their places on the streets where they lived. Contextualism is even less evident (and much less meaningful) in the Habenicht, Chapman and Bowers houses, all of which are free standing and detached and thus do not require further separation and disjunctiveness from within. Such is the power of formal manipulation to preclude involvement in other directions.

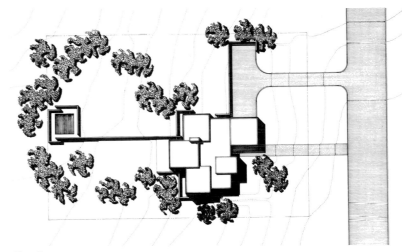
Site plan

Building Typologies (Zonolite
Advertisements), 1962–63

In association with
Norman A. Koglin

Perhaps the apogee of my Rudol-
phianist lionizing period, these
advertisements for masonry-fill
insulation were chock-full of
Rudolphian interlocking. Pin-
wheels push-pulled and click-
clicked their way out of my system
into the ad sections of the architectural mags of the day.

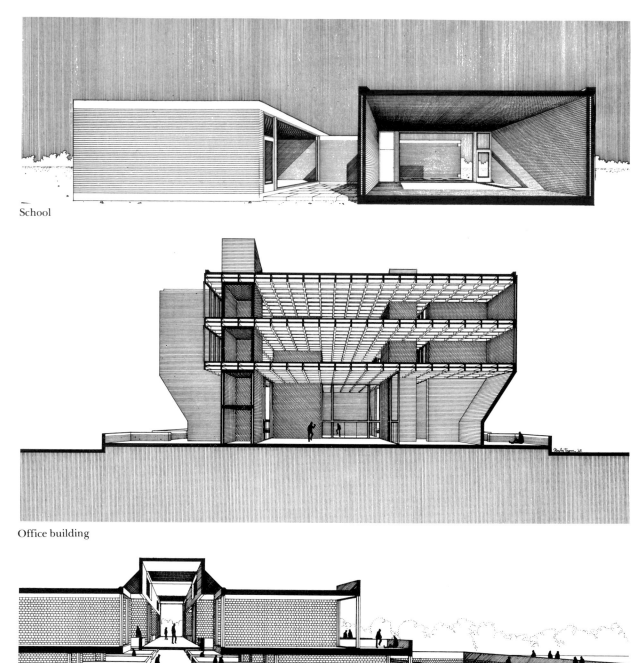

School

Office building

Commercial mall

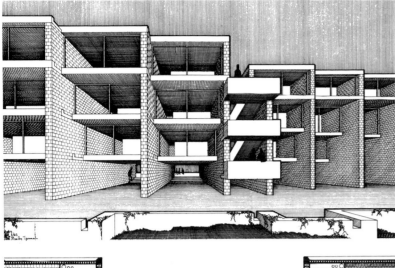

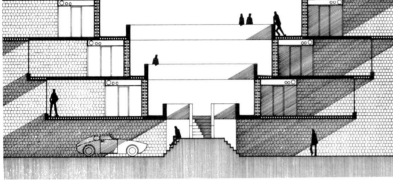

Motel

Office building

My most influential project in terms of codifying Brutalism—whose tenets I was then hard at work practicing—was a curious set of building types I cajoled into a kind of tentative reality if not tactile physicality. These building prototypes were actually nothing more than advertisements for the Zonolite Company demonstrating the usefulness of their product—masonry-fill insulations. They were a vehicle for showing off my newly matured Rudolphian style at its most abstract programlessness. The advertisements ran for several years—charts were even used to support the products' usefulness—but the hidden message was clearly involved in the architecture.

In the Zonolite advertisements I was able to organize my thoughts about the formal possibilities that lay in the designing of masonry buildings and to test devices I had been experimenting with earlier at Yale. They were a kind of post-postgraduate schooling in the very things I had been trained to do. They also showed my dissatisfaction with the pragmatics of practice since most of what they were intrinsically about, formally speaking, was too expensive in reality to produce.

At the end of the decade I modified my De Stijlian post-Cubist concepts with a new vocabulary of rounder corners, which signaled my growing interest in the sensuous. Rudolph's Endo Laboratories of 1962–64 (which influenced my Park Place Apartment Building Project) and several of his later single-family houses preceded this thinking of course. But the earlier portion of my work in this category was greatly influenced by Rudolph's student housing project at Yale and by James Stirling's early housing schemes with James Gowans and by the work of Ulrich Franzen and other architects who were trying to break away from the constrictions of canonical Modernism. Even Le Corbusier himself, in the Maisons Jaoul, materially altered his earlier concerns about the juxtaposition of Cartesian grids with the free plan.

Polemical purity in the context of Modernism itself was brought into question in the late 1950s and 1960s by Western European and American architects who were involved with materialization. In direct confrontation with them was a group of architects who were interested in dematerialization—and, in turn, abstraction. On both sides interests were intrinsically architectural in nature and unrelated to those of a third force that emerged toward the end of the 1960s: one

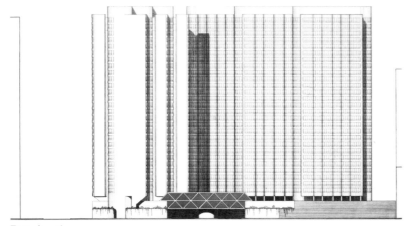

East elevation

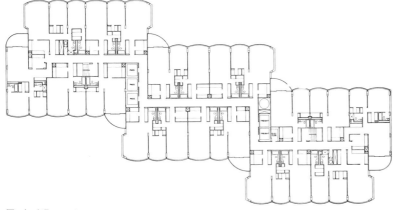

Typical floor plan

Park Place Apartment Building
Project, Chicago, Illinois, 1970–72

In collaboration with John Macsai
Assisted by John Haley, Karen
Thompson, Ralph Johnson
Structural engineer:
Wiesinger Holland
Mechanical and electrical
engineer: Wallace & Migdal

Reminiscent of Paul Rudolph's
Endo Laboratories project in its

replacement of rectangle with
curve, here repetition prevails and
this vertically striped behemoth
ultimately died of its own weight.
It is a curious mixture of pragmatic developmental notions unhap-
pily married to uneasy formal
manipulation—and the denial of
the Chicago grid doesn't help this
dinosaur.

that proposed a more socially egalitarian, advocacy-oriented architecture. A confrontation between these three essentially different attitudes was inevitable but until it happened I continued to ponder the familiar.

It was as if I were in an extended period of training, immersed in a deep study of the craft of architecture unfettered by any intellectual or emotional commitments. Chicago's fundamentalist Midwestern anti-intellectualism, which had so well supported Mies's Orwellian "non-speak," once again came to the rescue of those of us who would—as Mies had—simply peruse the craft itself. As long as we remained silent and refrained from examining too closely any cultural connections outside the art of architecture, we would be protected in ways that only a Chicagoan is protected.

But I began to understand Herbert Greenwald's rabbinical commitment to his work as a developer more clearly as I became aware of my own growing dissatisfaction with the intrinsics of architecture and started, ever so slightly, to become interested in cultural phenomena external to the discipline of architecture itself.

When Alberti wrote *Della Pittura* in 1463, he employed mathematics (the use of which has been overly stressed in Modernist interpretations of the treatise) primarily as a means to get at the content of the work—something he called *istoria*. In his book *Leon Battista Alberti on Painting* the art historian John R. Spencer states, "Unlike many theorists from the sixteenth century to our day Alberti does not believe that art is addressed pimarily to an elite; it is to reach all levels of society by the universality of its appeal."

Content. Such a simple word yet a word that was dense and opaque to someone trained to empty his work formally and structurally of content. After years of self-imposed intrinsic concerns I began to see the possibility of extrinsic ones finding their way into my work. But the potential for conflict in such a mixed marriage dissuaded me from immediately plunging into that disparate, dualistic world, for Modernist training is anything but temporal. Spatiality held sway as I rocked between Miesian and Corbusian beliefs, with my own real Platonic idealism yet to come.

Three: Geometric/Megastructure Phase 1958–1972

In some ways the work of my geometric/megastructure phase was the unavoidable result of my pedagogical pursuits with Josef Albers at Yale, which culminated in a series of formalist typologies I worked on for three years (1965–68) called The Formal Generators of Structure. The megastructure fever of the 1960s had much to do with my envisaging numerous projects as Orwellian fantasies. This period coincided precisely with my teaching tour at the University of Illinois, Chicago Circle Campus and my work was reinforced by numerous geometric studies developed by students of mine at the time. Buckminster Fuller was enjoying a resurgence of interest; the Metabolists (the Tange group at the University of Tokyo) were postulating visions in Tokyo Bay; Yona Friedman and other urbanists were writing papers and books—megathinking was in the air. I was particularly susceptible to this megathinking because of my geometric paintings and Formal Generators and also because my architectural output at the time was—as is the case with most young practices—"modest." Megastructures offered me the chance to clarify my thinking on the large issues of the day and to utilize my geometric interests in a timely manner. Although my fascination with large-scale visions continued for more than a decade, I looked to Mies not to megastructures for inspiration when the time came for me actually to build a "tall" building. In fact the only work completed in this métier were paintings and sculptures not buildings.

Paintings and Multiples, 1964–68

Typifying the mid-1960s American artistic shift from Pop to Op, these paintings and the modular sculpture extensions prefigure various architectural ordering devices I later developed as a basis for my own evolving megathinking. Hard-edged, they have soft content.

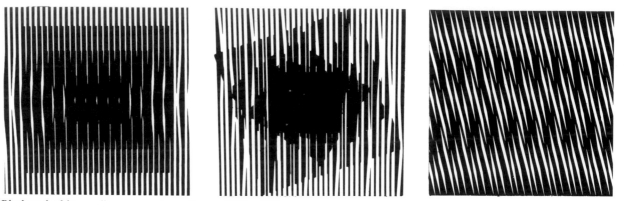

Black-and-white acrylic on masonite, each panel 30″ × 30″

Whenever architects have sought to "improve society" they have pictured themselves as pied pipers. In their desire to lead society to perfection they have used an important aspect of the craft of architecture itself: formalism. Formal manipulation has been a substantial force in the development of the classical aspect of architectural thought since Hellenic times.

By the mid-1960s attitudes connected with formal manipulation were very much in circulation in architectural academe, specifically at Cornell University where Colin Rowe, Robert Slutzky and, most significantly, John Hejduk were consolidating educational concepts that are even now at the root of architectural education in America. Platonic ideality was at the core of formal manipulation as it was taught at Cornell. Historical precedent formed the basis of the curriculum and measurement was used in making comparisons between pre-Modernist and Modernist masters alike. As the architectural historian George L. Hersey has shown us in his book *Pythagorean Palaces,* measurement and therefore proportion (the placing of value upon certain measurements as opposed to other measurements) are based on divine thought; they create, if you will, a false Utopia on earth.

Formalism thus used in the interests of furthering society's desire for perfection has always been in the mainstream of Hellenic thought and its architectural representation. The megastructure mania of the 1960s signaled a determinedly heroic return to formalism from the Brutalism of the late 1950s and early 1960s and yet was as self-involved as the latter. The traditional stylistic introvertedness inevitably led (along with the architects' genuine guilt feelings over the problems of mass housing) to a surge of advocacy position-taking at the end of the 1960s. While the literature on the megastructure movement has for the most part dealt with social concerns it has included sufficiently large doses of anonymity in its polemics to link the movement with the morality positions of architectural tastemakers like J. M. Richards, who titled a paper of his *The Condition of Architecture and the Principle of Anonymity.* (David Watkin has covered the whole subject of anonymity in his book *Morality and Architecture.*)

My own formalist concerns stemmed from the period when I painted in the style of Mondrian in the early 1950s. Subjected to the poetic pedagogy and color theories of Albers at Yale, my paintings became less compositional and more rational insofar as geometrical considerations replaced those of proportion. I was drawn to the rational concerns I felt existed in the paintings of such popular artists at the time as Victor Vasarely, Bridget Riley and Richard Anuskiewicz. This interest continued long after my exposure to Albers at Yale and culminated in a grant I received from the Graham Foundation for a trip to Europe in 1965. There I met the exciting new generation of Op art painters and theoreticians. It was a kind of confirmation trip.

After I returned from Europe I attempted to translate the rational concerns of Op art into a short, poetically inclined paper[1] and an architectural ordering device I ultimately called The Formal Generators of Structure.[2] A systems-based expansion of rectilinearly based geometry, the device professed to order syntactically those forms that it dealt with. Over a period of almost three years, with the assistance of Gordon Crabtree, a student of mine at the University of

Modsculp constructed of formica modules

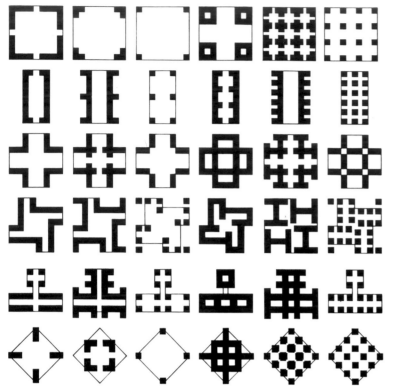

The six planar forms with columns, walls, buttresses

The Formal Generators of Structure, 1965–68

Drawings by Gordon Crabtree under the direction of the author

Architectonic extensions of my Albers-motivated paintings and sculptures, these forms work out in three dimension basic, orthogonally historical archetypes. After three years of moving toward bifocal vision, I felt it time to stop before the world of polyhydra took over.

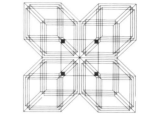

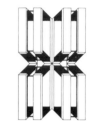

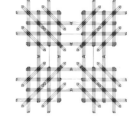
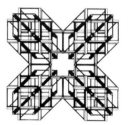

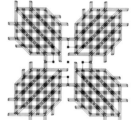
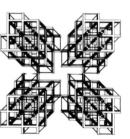

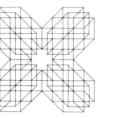

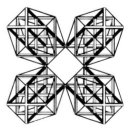

An example of a single set's development

Instant City, 1965–66

Assisted by Laurence Booth, James Nagle, Gordon Crabtree and Richard Franklin with consultation by Fazlur R. Khan

What I considered at the time to be a major breakthrough actually owes obvious debts to Gropius, Fuller, Tange and countless others who planned multiuses within a single overriding formal statement. Implicitly extending over freeways from coast to coast and more linear than Le Corbusier's plans for Algiers, it out-Orwells Cape Canaveral.

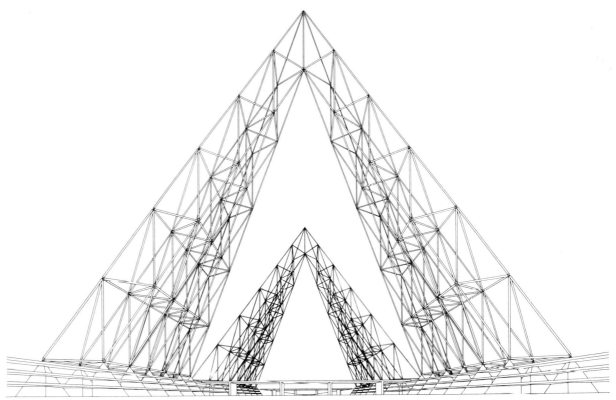

The structure unclad

Illinois, Chicago Circle Campus (where I was engaged in the teaching of similarly based matrix-oriented interests), some seventy-eight drawings of the most complex nature came into existence. As the 1960s became simultaneously more socially aware and systems oriented, my Formal Generators of Structure were very much in the spirit of the times.

Since by 1965 I had broken my partnership and was without sufficient work to occupy me—having at that time a distinct aversion to entering competitions—I found The Formal Generators of Structure a ready means for exploring my geometric and rational interests. Add to that the normal conceits of a young architect wishing to think big (particularly in light of the very small commissions I was then receiving) and one can see that my motivations for pursuing the structuring of rational forms were quite ordinary.

Once I had begun the abstract studies for The Formal Generators of Structure it seemed natural for me to move in a more concrete architectural direction, a direction that also conformed with the growing sense of rationalism in the air. In the mid-1960s I met Paolo Soleri, with whom I briefly taught a studio at the University of Illinois at Chicago Circle.

The structure clad

Photo of two models

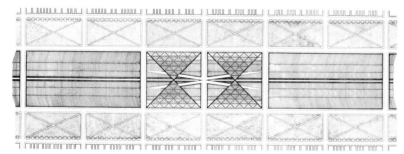

Site plan

This meeting, combined with my awe for Buckminster Fuller and a fortuitous meeting with the French sculptor (but architect-trained) Piotr Kowalski, set into motion a series of projects that propelled me into the world of megastructures.

I was carried along in that new and, for me at the time, exciting realm of large-scale thinking for seven years. My first project in this megastructure surge was Instant City, which I considered an architectural breakthrough and that was brought into existence through the very same copywriter at the very same advertising agency that had sponsored my earlier Rudolphian designs for prototypical structures. But I was bothered by the fact that the project seemed so different

Photo of two of them with a friend

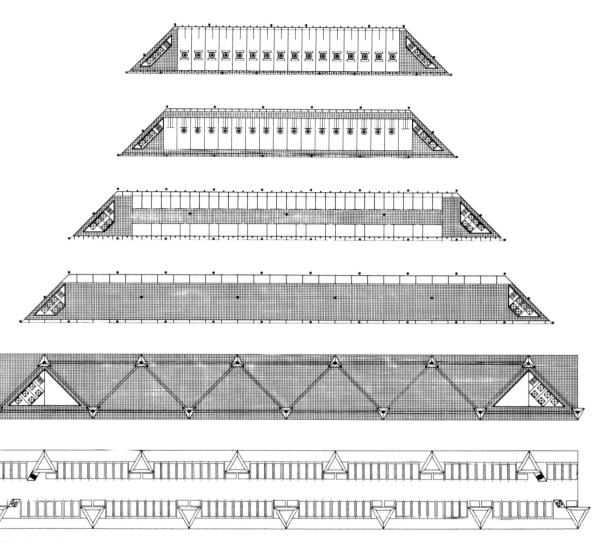

Multiple floor plans

from the things I had already done. I was of course still operating under the Zeitgeist theory of a lifelong pursuit of a single idea.

I shrugged off such guilt-laden concerns, however, and in 1967 plunged ahead on my next project, Urban Matrix, a visionary floating city for the Reynolds Aluminum Company. I was influenced by Fuller's megastructure projects, Yona Friedman's "sidewalks-in-the-sky" visions in Paris and the Tange group at the University of Tokyo—the so-called Metabolists. In 1971 the Swiss architect Justus Dahinden published a book called *Urban Structures for the Future,* adding to the architectural literature on megathinking. Earlier, in

1967, a pair of Russian architects named Shipkov and Shipkova had even proposed an Instant City look-alike for Leningrad in which it would have seemed more appropriate to see huskies pulling sleds than cars racing toward 1984.

The next step in my careening career of Utopian megavisions was taken at the prodding of my new-found Parisian sculptor-friend Piotr Kowalski. It was the development of a prototype floating airport, done with the cooperation of the Mitsubishi Heavy Industries Company of Tokyo. The project foundered but part of it lived on in another visionary affair called, amazingly enough, The Kingdom of Atlantis. A floating resort for a client who believed the location he had cho-

Urban Matrix, Chicago,
Illinois, 1967–68

Assisted by Maurice Girardi with
consultation by Fazlur R. Khan

Actually Instant City upside
down, the city seems to float in
Lake Michigan. The car is left
ashore and other pollutants are
shipped back from this floating,
cleansed object. Really a dense extension to center city, it has the
distinct advantage of being able to
have its cables clipped in the event
of a nuclear attack and its massive
(and presumably selected) segment of Chicago's inhabitants
floated away.

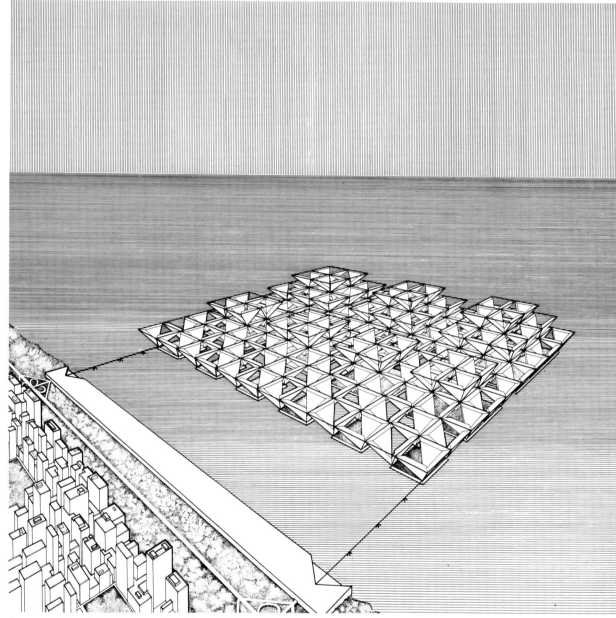

Axonometric with Chicago receding at lower left

Brobidignan Venetian canal and causeway

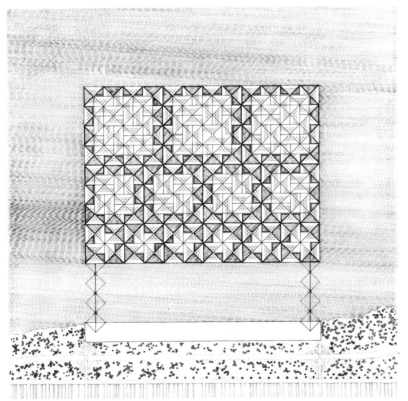

Site plan of one massive module

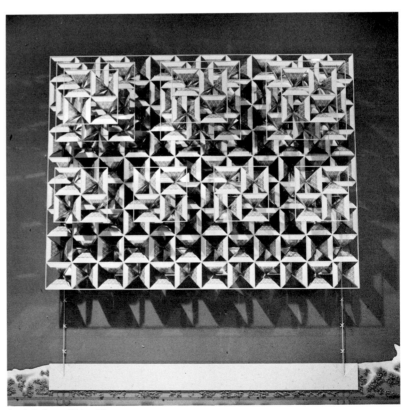

Aerial view of hive-likeness

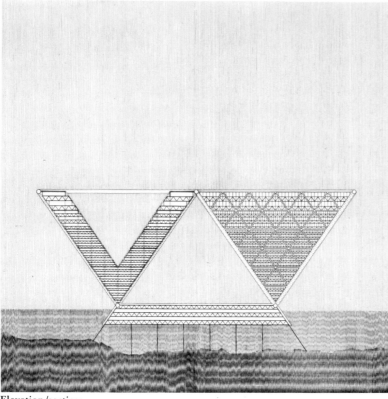

Elevation/section

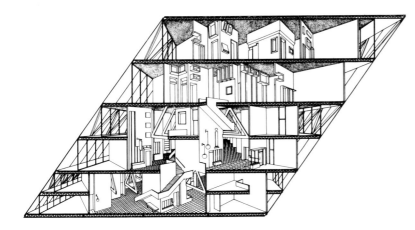

Interior axon (can you tell which way is up?)

sen in the Bahamas was precisely where the fabled Atlantis had gone under, the complex embraced the floating airport concept and added a series of rhomboid-shaped megamodules that contained hotels, recreational and port facilities, tennis courts, oil tanker refueling stations and other everyday floating conceptual elements.

My last proposal in the megaworld (though even now I occasionally hear from strange folk passing themselves off as potential clients who wish to build Instant City as housing in Calcutta or as resort hotels in Florida) was a hotel over a football stadium: Instant Football. The project became serious enough for a time to attract the attention of George Halas and the Chicago Bears, with whom I worked for about a year in 1972–73. Perhaps my greatest moment in this project came when Halas invited me to accompany him to New England to watch the Chicago Bears play the New England Patriots from the Owner's Box. The Bears lost the game and the project took a permanent turn for the worse. But I did manage to build one structure from this phase: a sixteen-foot high series of cube-octahedrons known as Modsculp. It perched majestically in the lobby of One Illinois Center just long enough to be documented before it was taken down.

This phase was all so incredibly heroic, but then heroism has always been a major factor in the tradition of Western architecture. Most Western buildings have been conceptually linked by their designers to earlier versions of similar origins; the Zeitgeist theory of the spirit of the age is only the beginning of the story. In the late 1960s attitudes relating to the nature of struggle began to surface in America but their appearance was certainly not regarded as cause for celebration. Rationalism and formalism still reigned supreme and Robert Venturi's *Complexity and Contradiction in Architecture,* which was published in 1966, though written in 1962, would have to wait fully ten years before it would be understood, let alone celebrated, and before an effort would be made to define its influence as a seminal work on American architecture. One more ingredient, however, was required to bring the architectural pot to a boil and that was the advocacy of minorities and the poor. This massive guilt complex about the elitist aspects of the architectural profession emerged in the late 1960s.

The 1960s thus rocked to a close from one side to another, always seeking synthesis yet at the same time avoiding the

The Kingdom of Atlantis (somewhere in the Bahamas), 1970

Assisted by Alan Olsen and John Hiltcher

Floating-resort complex and mid-Atlantic refueling station only begin to scratch at the pretensions involved here. Rhomboidal curtain-wallitis barely clads the Portmanesque hotel atrium. As with most cases of seasickness, all that is required for a cure is to get outside and smell the...refueling station (?).

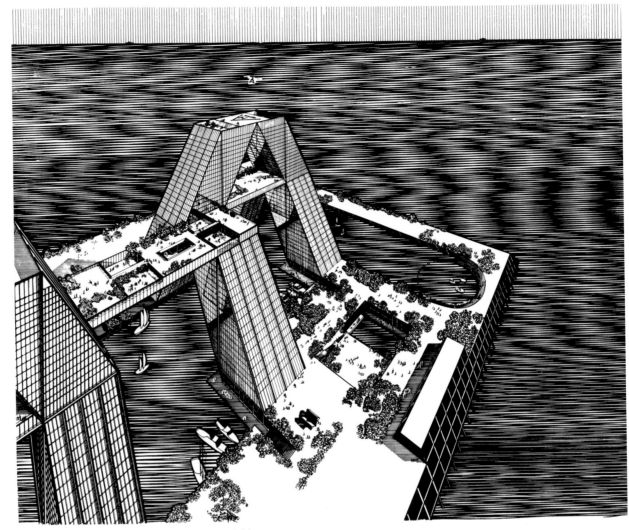

Aerial axonometric capturing many resort activities

exclusive study of one side or the other. While each side claimed to be the new spirit of the age neither would have much to do with the fashions and trends of the times. Architects continued to paraphrase Mies van der Rohe's "architecture as the will of an epoch translated into space" even as the 1960s headed toward its own tragic Viet Namese and inner-city revolutionary end. They played the pied piper to propositions of purity, ideality and perpetuity, partially because little in their backgrounds had prepared them to face issues with unhappy endings. The concept of struggle was yet to come.

View from end zone

Instant Football, Chicago,
Illinois, 1971–72

Assisted by Anthony Saifuki and
Bruce Thurman

Instant City (once again) disguised
as a hotel over a football stadium.

Capturing Atlantis's seasickness
component, the hotel affords a
dizzying view of the game below.
Warmed by fossil fuel and other
liquids, the spectators weave about
on account of the score and their
joy in not having to be among the

freezing patrons below them.
Summer rock concerts would up
the ante since paying hotel pa-
rents could keep an eye on their
grass-smoking, rock-fan, teenage
children.

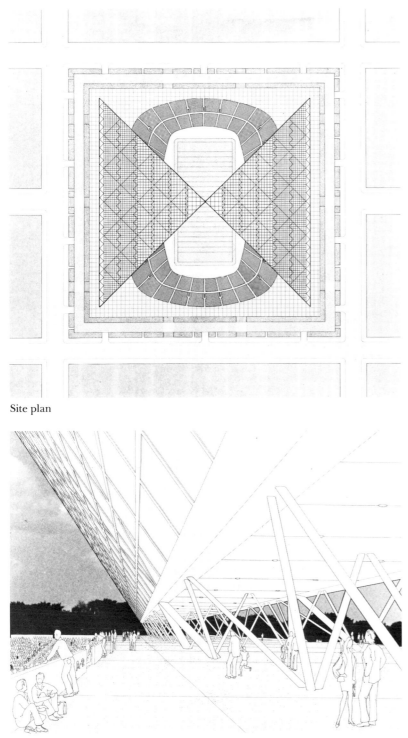

Site plan

View upon entering stadium

View of maintenance crew during off-season

View during half-time

1. *Juxtaposition vs. Judgment,* 1965

Before art stands discipline.

Discipline equips one with the ability
 to articulate those notions one always had.

Expressiveness in man can never be
 removed.

Indulgence of expressiveness engenders
 mystique.

Clarity and order are sought in existence.

There is no art without discipline.

Our fields of vision were secured early
 this century.

Refinement or reaction have been the
 issues ever since.

Now, for the first time, the phenomenology
 of vision suggests liberation.

The shifting base of our epoch is an
 insistently expanding technology.

No value judgment can deny the reality
 of this existence.

Man has the unique ability to extend
 beyond interpretation into existence.

Two Western rationalizations deal with
 the right angle.

One has been synthesized in religion
 as a spiritual universality.

In 1919, Mondrian paints three lozenges
 with rectangular fields passing
 through them.

While complying with orthogonal rationalizations,
 they imply both tension
 and extension.

The gestalt of the lozenge lies in that
 intersection of the diagonal with the
 orthogonal.

The gestalt of art lies in that intersection
 of one's own epoch and eternity.

2. *The Formal Generators of Structure,* 1967

Illustrations drawn by Gordon L. Crabtree under the author's direction

Initial research commissioned by the Keystone Steel and Wire Company of Peoria, Illinois

As the world of art, as well as that of science, comes to grips with "Systems Analysis" and "The Field Theory," it is necessary to for-

mally analyze certain two-dimensional man-made diagrams to ascertain their fundamental characteristics to better understand the role they will play in the forthcoming computerized world of networks and lattices.

Our fields of vision were secured early this century. Refinement or reaction have been the issues ever since. Now, for the first time, the constellating of the new optical qualities suggests liberation.

Two rationalizations of the Western world have focused on the unchanging qualities of the right angle. One has been synthesized in art as a formal universality in the form of the square. The other has been synthesized in religion as a spiritual universality in the form of the cross. The two visual symbols form the bases of a large part of those forms historically evolved by creative man.

The square, rectangle, cruciform, pinwheel, linked figure and lozenge are six of the more basic figures concerned with man's orthogonal preconceptions. Each, in its own way, while finite unto itself is linked with the others. The first five represent rectilinear notions while the sixth, the lozenge, introduces the diagonal phenomena.

By exploring four formal issues common to each of the six figures, certain characteristics of their respective geometries may be revealed:

Volumetric implications of planar extensions.
Axial properties of form reinforced by structure.
Architectonic extensions of axially reinforced figures.
Optical qualities of multiple axonometrics.

The square, as a discrete rectangle having four equal sides, has imaginary lines perpendicular to and through the center of its sides which form its bilaterally symmetrical properties. The plans of the churches at Santa Sophia in Istanbul and San Lorenzo are two examples of architects responding to the insistent geometry of the square. The four columns centered on each side of Mies's fifty-by-fifty house honor the axial properties of the figure while simultaneously contending with the asymmetrical superimposition of the core which lies in a state of shear relative to the structure. Albers's *Homage to the Twilight Square* of 1951 superimposes the notion of depth perspective onto the flat plane of multiple squares. Rowe and Slutzky note Kepes's commentary on figure-ground phenomena: "If one sees two or more figures overlapping one another and each one of them claims for itself the common overlapped part, then one is confronted with a contradiction of spatial dimensions. To resolve this contradiction one must assume the presence of a new optical quality. Max Bill's *White Element* extends the axes of the square to a position that when new points are connected a rotated square appears, while Mondrian's *Lozenge with*

Gray Lines of 1918 deals with the square as a field phenomena terminated by the lozenge and thus implying extension.

Vasarely extends the square toward three dimension while Bourgoin documents many of the "field" possibilities inherent in the two-dimensional square extended, connected and transformed. Clearly, the implications, extensions and potential deformations of the square have occupied a large segment of creative man's mind.

The appropriate form of the column relative to the cube is necessarily square. Thus, if the column expands or contracts in scale a similar residual space is left. The optical qualities obtained through equivocal figures have been supported historically by both "Schroder's reversible staircase" and "Thiery's Figure" which when seen in the light of Albers's constructions begin to shed light on that which is phenomenologically extendable. "Reye's configuration" (the juxtaposition of lines and planes which form a cube) contain as matrix the potential of extension to a three-dimensional network.

The square defined by planes continues the principle of trilateral axial reinforcement through extension into three dimension. In this case, the wall thickness is such that through planar termination the negative space of the opening is also a square. Thus, while any wall thickness might have been employed, similar performance can be had only if the termination of the planes were to form a square. The architectonic extensions of the walled square demonstrate the spatial implications of trilateral symmetry as defined by clusters of planes constellating into L-shaped elements.

The buttressed sparse square, curiously, begins to imply the cruciform which, as the square, is bilaterally symmetrical. This is natural since the form of four planar buttresses when disposed about a square necessarily resemble a cruciform. It should be noted, however, that the juxtaposition of multiple buttresses containing a cube imply the cube rather than the cruciform.

The rectangle, architecturally speaking, has as its formal origins the Gothic style. The linear characteristics of this style reinforce a single axis, the termination of which has continued to be of considerable difficulty. The plan of the chapel of Saint Stephen simply terminates the parti after five structural bays while that of Sainte Chapelle in Paris weights one end of the axis by actually closing the other. Notre Dame, while similar to Sainte Chapelle, recognizes a minor axis perpendicular to the nave. If one assumes that the square is simply a discrete rectangle, then elongated forms of similar geometry may well contain similar properties. Thus, illustrations herein articulate the rectangle composed of two squares, weighting one axis more than the other due to the obvious effects of elongation.

The rectangle, like the Gothic parti, has major and minor axes: thus when the figure is extended into space, the major axial termi-nation becomes bilaterally symmetrical (similar to the cube). Thus, the longitudinal planar extensions are of the same proportion as the sides of the rectangle. That a close relationship exists between the rectangle and the square is inevitable.

While the columned sparse rectangle and the walled sparse rectangle focus on the linear aspects of the Gothic parti, the buttressed sparse rectangle three-dimensionally wraps the minor centroid so that while the major axes in all three cases deal with subjective visual penetration through the opening at either end of the form a feeling of compression is established in the buttressed rectangle articulating its minor axial properties.

As the rectangle is an extension of the square in terms of its being the agglomeration of two squares, the cruciform is the agglomeration of three, two-square rectangles mutually and simultaneously disposed about the "x," "y" and "z" axes. It, as well as the square, is trilaterally symmetrical in three-dimensional terms to the extent that the negative space achieved by the juxtaposition of the four axonometrics form a cruciform as well.

Historically, the plan of the chapel at San Spirito in Florence is an interesting demonstration of the transition from the Gothic to the Renaissance (or indeed the rectangle to the cruciform). San Spirito, while cruciform in plan, has its nave slightly elongated thus combining the rectangle and the cruciform in an interesting manner. The history of classical city planning has utilized the cruciform potentialities such as Versailles and the overall plan for San Pietro's. J. Bourgoin has shown the use of this figure in Arabian art decoration. His *Les Éléments de l'art Arabe* shows many permutations of the cruciform and other bilaterally symmetrical figures.

The cruciform structured by columns continues the principle of the cube structured by columns. The architectonic extensions of the cruciform are most appropriately made with a flemish bond as this is also a cruciform in organization. The negative spaces resulting from the walled and buttressed containers have protruding and receding spaces reinforcing the cruciform notion as well. It should be noted that the proportion of the angle-shaped containing planes, while having similar sides, define a 2:1 axial entry to the center square, this proportion being consistent with the 2:1 three-rectangle juxtaposition forming the structure of the basic figure.

Mies's Brick Villa of 1923 demonstrates a loose compositional way of dealing with the pinwheel, while the plan of Wright's Suntop House of 1939 shows a more compact organization of this figure. There have been many attempts to articulate the shearing aspects of the pinwheel in the plastic arts. Albers's constructions have emphasized this quality through the weighting of lines. The Rietveld House at Utrecht of 1923–24 shows some of the three-dimensional possibilities of this parti.

The pinwheel is composed of a series of rectangles the juxtaposition of which constellate about a pinwheel or swastika figure in such a way that the cruciform, the central negative space formed by the gathering of the four axonometric extensions also forms a pinwheel. The abstract pinwheel figure is a study in the distortions possible in the logical graphic notation in this figure. More than the square, rectangle or cruciform, this parti justifies the four axonometric postulate for showing all faces at once. This is a result of the parti not being symmetrical (at least in the sense one thinks of the square or cruciform).

The pinwheel structured by columns establishes a cubic lattice, only the termination points of which define the pinwheel form. The walled pinwheel is composed of both solid and void L-shaped forms extending from the planar four walls. The buttressed pinwheel continues the shearing phenomena of this figure into a complex network of channel-shaped containers, the negative spaces of which are also buttressed with channel-shaped transparent planes.

The linked figure is the constellation of perpendicularly oriented rectangles linked and then extended into three-dimensional space. If one considers the extension of the lateral elements of Blenheim Palace in Oxfordshire they then form a linked figure with the central hall of the Palace. The Inland Steel Building in Chicago by Skidmore, Owings and Merrill is a clear demonstration of the figure itself with minimum understanding of its axial properties (which might have otherwise created a more appropriate human penetration through entry).

The lozenge while having historic roots not unlike the five earlier parti, nonetheless has quite different axial properties. Assuming the square-cube to have axes perpendicular to its sides establishes its formal generators. If the square is tilted 45 degrees and the "x" and "y" axes also turned 45 degrees, the square simply becomes a square turned on its side with no particular unique properties. However, if when the square is turned 45 degrees the "x" and "y" axes remain in their original position, a completely new set of optical rules occurs. This was never made more clear historically than in the work of two members of the Dutch movement De Stijl, Mondrian and van Doesburg. During the years 1918 and 1919 Mondrian did three lozenge paintings where only the periphery of the canvas was tilted. The interior field remained in a vertical and horizontal position. Van Doesburg's reply to this was "Elementarism" (a humanistic introduction) which in his painting of 1924 and 1925 the periphery remained orthogonal and the interior field was tilted. The Mondrian postulate has been clearly extended in John Hejduk's Diamond House of 1965.

It should be noted that the axial properties of the lozenge are orthogonal while the figure itself is the extension into space on the diagonal. One of the curious optical results of this juxtaposition is the completely different way in which axonometric extensions occur. The disposition of these paradoxical sets of principles establishes a new methodology of extension, marrying many of the principles of the square, cruciform and pinwheel but simultaneously establishing a new visual language.

The square, rectangle, cruciform, pinwheel, linked figure and lozenge through great repetition have, on occasion, uplifted the creative mind to establish an order clearly defining the nature of these forms. The Golden Rectangle and le Modulor are but two of the many efforts in this milieu. One must assume that the three-dimensional, topological extensions possible in the future will establish yet another set of values defining the nature of those spaces utilizing the basic properties of these six parti.

Four: Advocacy/Socially Conscious Phase 1963–1978

The work of this fifteen-year phase generally illustrates problem-solving interpretations of the 1960s and specifically that of Chicago pragmatism. One atypical project spans almost the entire phase—the Bangladesh Polytechnic Institutes. Style, structural expressionism—all my earlier interests—do not form a part of the thought process of this stage. They somehow seemed inappropriate to an architecture emanating from post-Team-Ten attitudes and other problem-solving postures of the time. I applied the same rationale of practicality to housing not connected with inner-city problems. I was not alone in doing this—Davis and Brody as well as Conklin and Rossant excelled at it in New York City and Harry Weese (and later Ben Weese) made pragmatic housing a distinct part of their practice in Chicago. Rehabilitation—in particular the development of "forensic" architectural neighborhood clinics—seemed the suitable thing for me to do since I had contacts with neighborhood organizations through my low-rise, low-cost housing projects. Much of the pragmatism here is really thinly veiled capitalism supporting private development geared to consumer marketing. This was the last phase of my work executed "within the times" inasmuch as I was beginning to feel dissatisfied with what I was doing.

The pragmatism of the late 1960s was in many ways a denial of the hermeticism associated with intrinsic architecture—that is, architecture with a capital A. This pragmatism did not, however, result in a total misuse of architectural talents since it required architects to react responsibly to urban conditions. But unfortunately this responsible attitude also manifested itself in an overly endowed functionalism, in housing projects—more often federally funded than not—that missed the chance to respond contextually to the American fabric. Instead—often as a product of urban renewal (America's amazing way of ridding itself en masse of whatever traditions had accrued)—new developments arose from wastelands with little, if any, context left.

Despite all these problems, which I recognize in retrospect, I now see one positive development as far as my own work was concerned. The opportunity to stop and reflect on the whole concept of responsibility had a profound effect on my thinking, far more profound than I was aware of at the time, and I became aware of the responsibilities of communicating with a larger audience than the one of architectural cognoscenti (housing has a great ability to temper architectural introvertedness). In the late 1960s the urgency of post-World-War II, post-Team-Ten functionalism was made all the more poignant by the new student attitudes toward egalitarianism in America, which had resulted in part from America's increasing involvement in Viet Nam. American architects examined moderate-income, inner-city housing with the hope of providing new housing models that would upgrade urban living conditions. Of course the Utopian attitudes of Modernism helped to fuel such attitudes.

In my own work three types of projects dealing with these pressing problems came into focus within a very short time. The first were the housing and vocational training institutions I designed in what was then East Pakistan. The second were the low-cost housing studies, forensic clinics and large-scale works contending with the subject of mass housing in the inner city. And the third were the inevitable (if not entirely gratifying) by-the-book pragmatic housing projects, which, though they may have lacked social concerns, owed their existence indirectly to my low-cost housing projects. Here in this phase at last I could give form to my current interests in social relevancy, at the same time using the responsible problem-solving methods of Modernism. For many of us it was a really exciting moment in architecture, one in which we felt we could provide appropriate responses to the issues of the day. It spawned projects by well-intentioned architects such as Louis Sauer, Marquis and Stoller, Davis and Brody and many others.

In 1964 Paul Rudolph and I were invited to East Pakistan by Muzharul Islam, a former classmate of mine at Yale and a very close friend. His purpose was to introduce us to key government officials in the hope that they might ask us to do work there. He was concerned about the education of the architecture students of his country, whom he felt were being inadequately trained by United States A.I.D.-connected institutions such as Texas A. & M. Rudolph and I met in Rome in July, 1964, and flew to Dacca, in what was then East Pakistan, now Bangladesh. The trip was an eye-opening experience for me and I think for Rudolph as well. I had never before been exposed to the depths of poverty I observed in that country. And neither had I been exposed to a practice of architecture which required architects to design everything from windows and their mechanisms to chairs (Graphic Standards and Knoll International did not exist in Dacca) and to concern themselves with the environment including matters of not only orientation and movement of air but fungus, algae and mold—common conditions in a deltaic alluvial plane, in this case the rain forest of the Asian subcontinent.

Rudolph was quickly commissioned to complete an agricultural university in Mymensingh, a small village north of Dacca with several modern buildings, among them a little-known, banal, wrongly oriented building by Richard Neutra. Rudolph, Islam and I traveled by jeep through the monsoon rains to the unfinished campus, which was sited along the Brahmaputra River. I'll never forget sitting on the verandah of the guest house talking late into the night with Islam and listening to Rudolph in his room swatting at all the creepy-crawlers with his shoe. The whole trip was amazing: the dinner parties on board a launch on the Ganges, the visits to Lahore, Rawalpindi and Islamabad in West Pakistan (now Pakistan) and the continuous meetings, tea parties and dinners with government officials concerned with the environment.

The next year (1965) a mission from the World Bank went to Dacca to discuss expanding the vocational training insti-

Five Polytechnic Institutes for the World Bank and the People's Republic of Bangladesh at Bogra, Barisal, Pabna, Rangpur and Sylhet, Bangladesh, 1966–80

In association with Muzharul Islam, Vastukalabid, architect

Assisted by John Hartman, Judith May, Ida Baird, Mohamed K. Shaheedullah and Messrs. Shafi and Nurul-ullah and staff in Dacca, Bangladesh

Photography: Muzharul Islam

A series of vocational training institutions in the unrelenting climate—bereft of Shakespearian comic relief—of a poverty-stricken country on the verge of revolution. A major lesson in "total design," it fails nonetheless, I now see, to provide any architectural options to the existing cultural conditions—rather it supplants such aspirations with straight-faced, problem-solving Modernism.

Exterior view

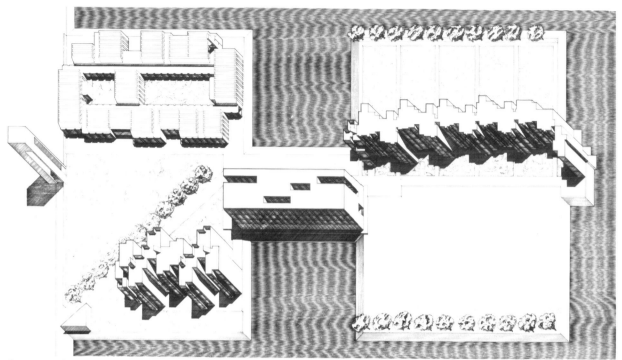

Axonometric

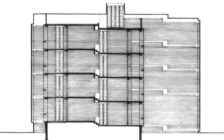

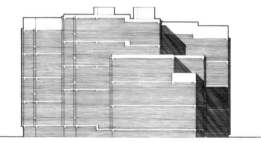

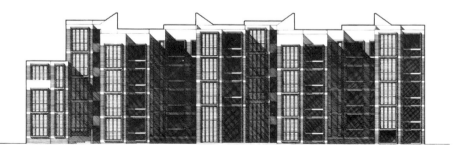

Elevation section

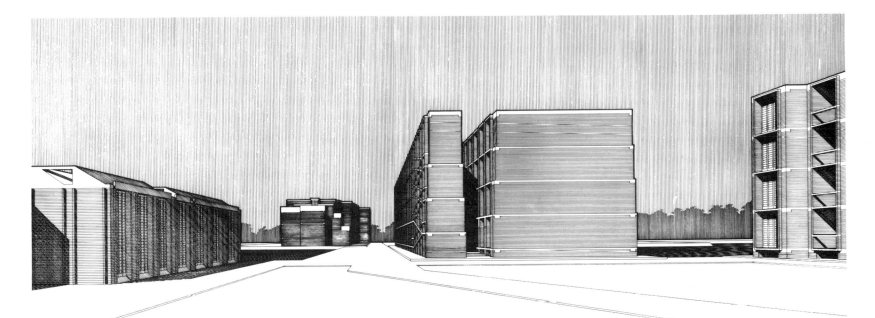

Perspective

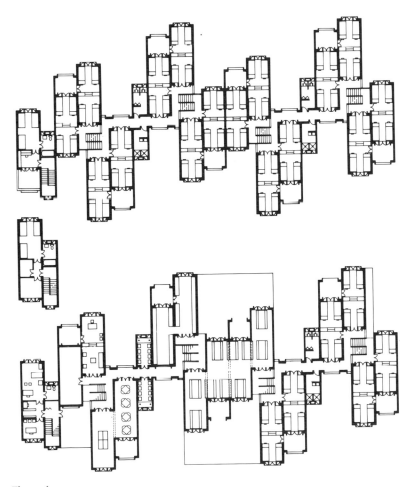

Floor plan

tutes into polytechnic institutes capable of producing a cadre of men with certificates between high school and university levels who could supervise the jute, cotton, gas and other technologies. This team met with Muzharul Islam (who by this time had left government service for private practice) and offered him the commission with the proviso that he collaborate with either a Western European or American architect. Islam recommended me. I was asked to present my credentials at the World Bank in Washington, D.C., and then the work began—but not before I met the official at the World Bank responsible for the project, Sergei Kadleigh. His concern for the people of Bangladesh was far more intense than what one might expect from a World Bank bureaucrat and his unflagging contribution to the project was extraordinary indeed.

The polytechnic project had perhaps its greatest effect on me as a consequence of Muzharul Islam's insisting that I live with the Bengalis and spend as little time as possible with the American community in Dacca. I ate the Bengalis' food and drank their water, got dysentery and was cured and became acclimated to the local conditions. Islam also made sure that I approached the problem of designing for his people in a way that would bring lessons of Western logic to the young architects of East Pakistan well beyond those inherent in the buildings themselves. This in turn prompted me to become

Exterior view

aware of the needs of my own people and of the way architecture is practiced in America, where a generally high level of sophistication in the discipline is taken for granted. In a country such as Bangladesh, in which poverty is a way of life, massive expenditures on design products simply cannot be taken for granted. It was an enormously rewarding experience that even now influences my thinking.

One event of staggering proportions occurred that I could never have anticipated. In the course of my many trips in the late 1960s to Dacca and the five village sites for the vocational training centers, I was conscious of a growing restlessness among the Bengalis. Even my good friend Islam, an architect held in great esteem in his country, became involved with the growing agitation toward independence, holding meetings regularly in his office with the academic, professional and political intelligentsia.

In March, 1971, East Pakistan struck out to become an independent nation and met resistance from the central government in West Pakistan. Thus the struggle for an independent Bangladesh began. Along with others who had conspired toward this end, Islam fled the country to Calcutta, where he settled with his family during the struggle for liberation. Meanwhile his son Rafique, the renowned structural engineer Fazlur Khan and I met in Chicago to form the Bangladesh Defense League whose purpose was to raise money for the liberation struggle in America. During the summer of 1971 our client in Dacca requested that I come to Dacca to work on Islam's projects. So (fearfully) in Sep-

Exterior view

tember, 1971, I went to Dacca to have a look. But after being searched at both the airport and the hotel in Dacca at gunpoint and with a bayonet and having materials of the project commandeered by the army, I felt the project should be suspended. I told my client this, enumerating other incidents I had observed in Dacca. I thought the army was attempting to reduce the country to an agriculturally based society by systematically killing off its intelligentsia. Our office was then notified that if work on the polytechnics did not resume, its members would be considered enemies of the country.

Obviously I could no longer work in East Pakistan and so I left the country, flying first to Bangkok and then rerouting myself to Calcutta where I met with Islam and members of the revolutionary government. I then notified the govern-

ment of East Pakistan and the World Bank that I was resigning my commission and simultaneously held a press conference.[1] I returned to Chicago, where, three months later, in December, 1971—after the liberation struggle had ended in the founding of the People's Republic of Bangladesh—I received a cable from the new government reinstating both myself and the projects.

It was all an extraordinary episode, particularly since there had been no precedent in my life for handling such things. It gave me new insights into the moral and responsible ways with which to deal with the problems of a clientele that normally never reaches an architect: the poor. Thus when I began to work on inner-city projects for community organizations in Chicago, I found I was better prepared to cope

Woodlawn Gardens, Chicago, Illinois, 1963–69

Originally in collaboration with Norman A. Koglin

Assisted by Richard Rothman, Thomas Hirsch and Richard Lindblade

An experiment in a 504-unit low-rise, high-density urban housing, this project finally got under way in 1968 after I had been to Dacca several times. It was built on the community's demand to provide housing similar to suburban lily-white solutions. With piggy-back (two over one) stacked maisonettes over flats, this not-for-profit low-rent housing would have made more sense if it had had some form of ownership position.

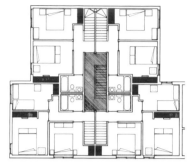

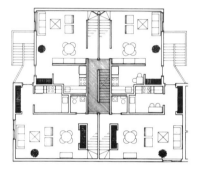

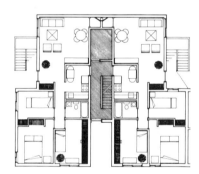

Floor plans

Mid-rise housing for the elderly

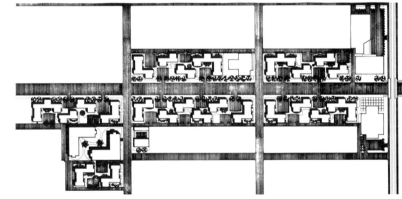

Site plan

Low-cost Housing Studies for
the Chicago Dwelling Association,
1965–66

Assisted by Laurence Booth,
James Nagle and
Richard Franklin

Taut studies emanating from the
Woodlawn Gardens experience,
these high-density housing studies
for the Chicago Dwelling Association never were realized but they
formed the basis for pragmatic
builder-development yet to come.

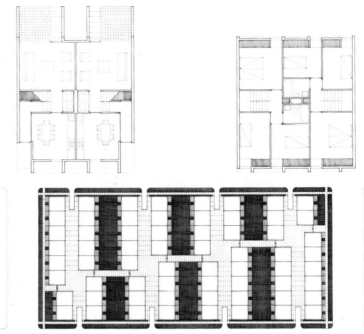

Quadriplex piggy-back housing module plan and section

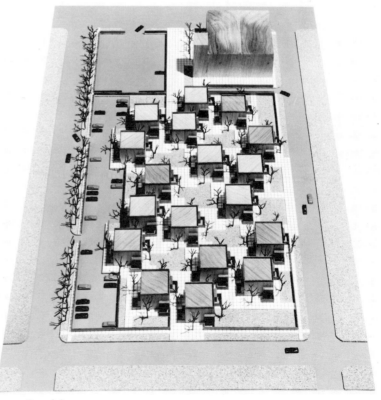

Photo of model

than I would have been had I never had the Bangladesh
experience.

Because of my work with these community organizations—primarily through the offices of the Maremont
Foundation, the creation of a wealthy Chicago industrialist
interested in rehabilitation—I became involved in rehabilitation projects and forensic clinics and in a large housing
project for The Woodlawn Organization (TWO). In looking
back I can now see that those of us who were grappling with
housing problems were limited by our very zealotry. There
was no humor in our work and we used none of the traditional weapons of architecture—symbolism, decoration,
contextualism. The desire to resolve need in and of itself
seemed to us sufficient to justify the projects that came off
our drawing boards throughout the decade 1965–75.

Problem solving becomes most depressing, however, in
housing projects that have little, if any, relation to social
problems—the standard capitalistically based housing projects of entrepreneurship. I was involved in such projects of
course and they are among the least rewarding experiences
of my career. But they did lead me away from functionalist
concerns back, for a time, to formalist interests. Even without
social concerns housing still seemed valid to me. But this was
before Robert Venturi's *Complexity and Contradiction in Architecture* really took hold on the impoverished condition of
architecture. Post-Modernism was just a gleam in a few ar-

Prairiebrook, a Low-rise
Housing Complex, Palatine,
Illinois, 1974–78

Assisted by Anthony Saifuku,
Robert Fugman and David
Woodhouse together with
Rafique Islam

A moderate-income project for
IHDA (Illinois Housing Development Authority), the project
combines the campus-planning
modularity of Woodlawn Gardens
with the perimeter parking of a
Greenbelt solution—thus no new
ground is broken in suburban
housing. Devoid of decoration, its
sparseness is somewhat amelio-
rated by a modest Walden Pond
approach to landscaping and
water systems.

Photo view of garden apartment module

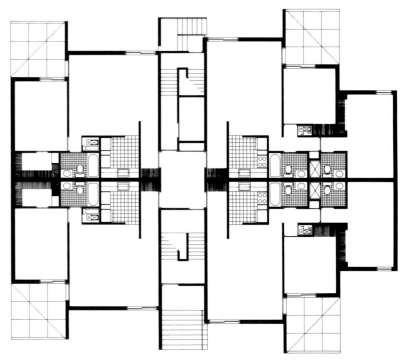

3-story garden apartment module

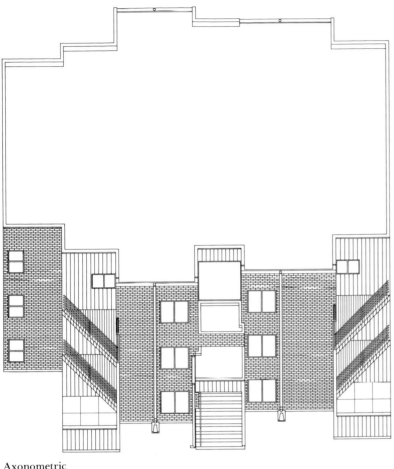

Axonometric

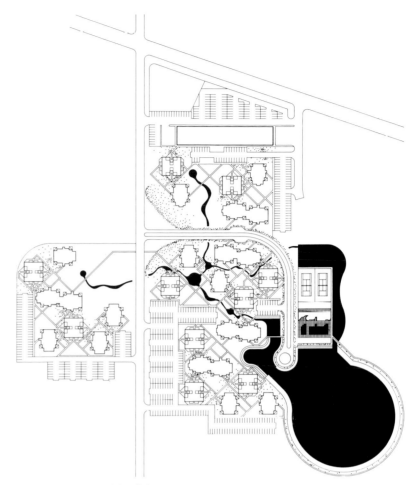

Site plan (Phase I, 320 units)

tists' eyes and most architects were continuing to spew forth schismatic Modernist concerns.

As in the past I had always managed to avoid being hired by clients in arenas of interest with which I had grown disenchanted, I now systematically cut off developers who wanted to commission me to do housing bereft of elaboration and embellishments. I sensed a dead end in this kind of housing and felt the need of renewal, and I know of no more meaningful way to achieve this in architecture than to work with clients who are the actual users of the buildings in question.

At about this time I began to feel that my rapid involvements with Miesianism, Brutalism, megastructures and social consciousness—and the fact that I hadn't picked any one of them for a lifetime career—rendered me unfit to practice architecture in a single-minded fashion. This seeming lack of

tenacity or commitment to a particular direction bothered me, needless to say, since most of my peers were indeed being single-minded in their approach to architecture. But after all, one-dimensionality—any direction will do, I suppose— is at the root of Platonic ideality, which, in turn, is at the basis of architecture. And while the freneticism of the times augured against the taking of any one direction architects themselves, heedless of the times, split off in pursuit of their several interests. Although the decade 1965–75 may have signaled the end of the generation of revolutionaries that had won (a full half-century earlier to be sure) the massive battle against neoclassicism, it also witnessed the lasting influence of these recently deceased warriors on architects seeking the Zeitgeist spirit of the age. The specters of Le Corbusier, Mies van der Rohe, Louis Kahn and Alvar Aalto continued to dissuade architects from responding to the trends of the times. Modernism remained all-powerful, but in America it seemed to become increasingly perverse.

1. *Text Presented at Press Conference in Calcutta, India, September, 1971*

I am an architect. I am not a political person.

Five years ago, in 1966, the Government of Pakistan in cooperation with the World Bank commissioned me to design five polytechnic institutes at Barisal, Bogra, Pabna, Rangpur and Sylhet in what was then East Pakistan. In order to rationally establish design criteria (which were not available at that time) my firm developed an extensive master plan organizing data on climatology, sociology, meteorology, seismology, natural resources, construction methods, building codes and standards, labor and material rates, etc. I came to know the country very well. Over these five years, in conjunction with my work, I made sixteen trips to Dacca and other parts of the country, developing many lasting friendships with the people of the country.

As of March, 1971, all five projects were substantially under construction. The events of March 25 and subsequent to that time caused me to have personal doubts as to my continued involvement with the work. I conveyed these doubts to the World Bank. However, I wished to witness, first hand, the conditions to properly assess whether or not I could continue. Since I felt it necessary, I went to Dacca September 18 and spent one week reviewing the conditions and attendant problems to the development of the polytechnics. Dacca is not the same city I knew it to be. There is a level of fear that makes it difficult to discuss even the most mundane technical problems. The martial law authorities have created an atmosphere through threats, searches and check-points that, in combination with the presence everywhere of police and the army, is tantamount to a "police state."

The polytechnic projects are very dear to me. Nonetheless, it seems to me that some level of moral judgment must be exercised with respect to offering my professional services to a government that forces people to work by threatening them that they will be an enemy of the government, with its attendant implications, if they do not work. This is not my idea of "normalcy."

I have, this day, cabled the Government of Pakistan and the World Bank that, under the terms of my contract, I am exercising the termination clause therein. I do not wish, nor have I the right to ask people to supervise and engage in the construction of buildings I am responsible for and risk their physical well being, indeed their very lives, in the process.

I have no intention of working for a military government with its attached implications. Moreover, I will never again travel to East Pakistan. Lastly, when the country is free and self-determining I would wish to visit and hopefully work in Bangladesh for I have come to love these people and their country very much.

I am an architect. I am also a human being.

Five: Manipulated Modernist Phase 1971–1981

This phase is exactly the kind of innocuous extension of Mies's Modernism one might expect from a "Chicago architect." The New York Five (particularly Charles Gwathmey and Richard Meier) were a strong influence on me during the decade of this phase (they still are). Since I knew Gwathmey and Meier personally in addition to knowing their work I found the transition to their style easy to make. Manipulated (if small-scale) Modern architecture was right at home in Chicago. It was the sort of architecture I was trained educationally and experientially to do well and I felt comfortable with it as a design methodology. It had pedigree and class; like Rice Krispies it could not harm or help, but best of all, it was "correct." It had a style and it also had "style." It was the architectural mainstream of the 1970s and I knew it. Gwathmey and Meier did it; Harry Wolf of North Carolina did it; neo-Corbusians in New York and neo-Miesians in Chicago did it—all of them did it, and most of them better than I, but I did it too. It provided a lot of room within which to manipulate situations and it offered the possibility for sensuousness (the kind I detected in the work of Eric Mendelsohn and others of the soft-corner depression-Moderne era). It was Mies's free plan combined with the free spirit of the 1970s and it worked.

Apartment Remodeling Project,
Chicago, Illinois, 1971

Assisted by Anthony F. Saifuku

The first in a series of projects for
the 1970s Now Generation, this
apartment was in part remodeled
to accommodate disco parties.
Curvy reminiscences of 1920s
Modernity are used in much the
same way soft-corner depression-Moderne forms were
used—as an escape from the
harsh realities of the world.

View of living/dining area

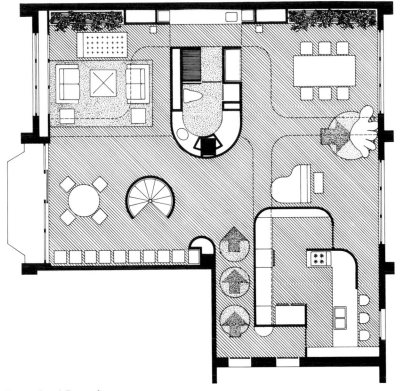

Lower level floor plan

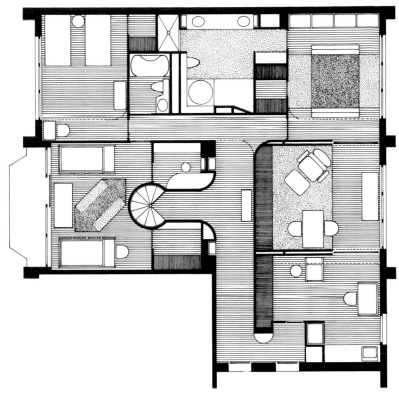

Upper level floor plan

Although on the surface this category of my work may appear to be stylistically connected with schismatic Modernism the roots of this phase in fact lie in client interpretation. It is the beginning of the end of image-making for me and the start of content-oriented designing, in which the individual client in all his or her idiosyncratic glory is reflected.

Most of the work is residential in nature, wherein programmatic responsiveness is quickly followed by idiosyncratic elaboration. Even so, manipulated Modernism is the crutch I used to hobble with through this period, unsure of just where I was going but always ready to recall where I had been.

Many of these residential projects were designed for the Now Generation of the 1970s, a generation not entirely unlike that of the 1920s, with its Moderne buildings and accouterments symbolic of the modish and the craze to be fashionable. Unlike most architects I was not in a hurry to condemn certain fashions and trends as déclassé once the canonical Modernity of the 1950s slipped into the disco drama of ar-

chitectural anagrams of the 1970s. I sensed, rather, the opportunity to use style to comment upon the nature of those frenetic times while still servicing the formal conceits of my clientele. These two attitudes quickly merged into a new style that melded client pretentions with the sleek chic of proto-High-Tech, itself an amalgam of the Bauhaus and all-American fashion (only this time the imagery didn't need Platonic perfection since the cult of individuality discouraged any single response to the times).

Just as Mondrian loved the American jazz and boogie-woogie of the late 1930s and early 1940s, I loved the American disco moves of the early 1970s. To me they were an expression of the shaking off of guilt from the late, less-than-great, Viet Nam 1960s.

Miniskirts worked well with minithoughts about mini-buildings. The single-family house replaced Modernism's noble buildings, ushering in a new brand of hero and heroine: the individual in his or her *very* individual house. A late-night TV replay of the 1930s movie *New Times,* it kept

Ski Lodge Project, Vail, Colorado, 1972

Hard on the heels of the disco apartment comes this après-ski chalet in the ticky-tacky Tyrolean plastic ambience of Vail, Colorado. Billiard room and amphitheater for nude sunbathing are among the several wonders of this unbuilt project. Gwathmey-esque simplistic geometric forms merge with Miesian fenestration, all attempting to legitimize architecturally the protophallic phase yet to come. Moreover this metaphorical mask is completed by Midwestern materiality (cedar siding).

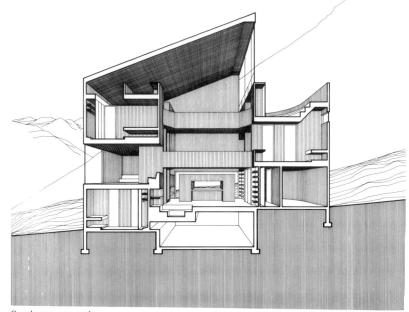

Section perspective

our minds off the more serious reminders of the late 1960s. This escapism ultimately failed, of course. Even the modishness of 1970s architecture was only a superficial comment on the times, not a deep emotional reaction that could in any way supplant the poignancy of post-Viet Nam America.

For me, the Deathly Mask of Silence of Tafuri-interpreted Modernism offered a means of commenting on the times. This Modernist technique was image-making in the sense that while it seemed to hide its culture on the one hand it commented on it on the other. Through this dichotomy I slowly became aware of the nature of the conflict between ideality and pragmatism, between the normal desire for Platonic perfection and the secret desire to rupture. The schisms of the times, boiling beneath the surface, were ready to erupt in my architecture, through which I wished to explain, if not change, these times. Though canonical Modernity is at the core of the formal manipulation of this phase, the notion of rupture, which represents my dissatisfaction with the times, manifests itself and the nature of struggle replaces my ideas about Platonic ideality. In the 1979 monograph on the work of Michael Graves, Alan Colquhoun writes that "the fragmentation of [Graves's] buildings suggests the presence of natural obstacles to conceptual completeness and the ina-

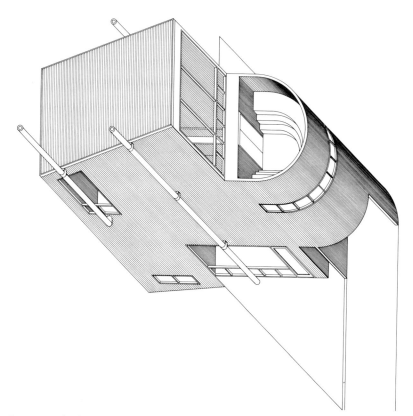

Axonometric view of exterior

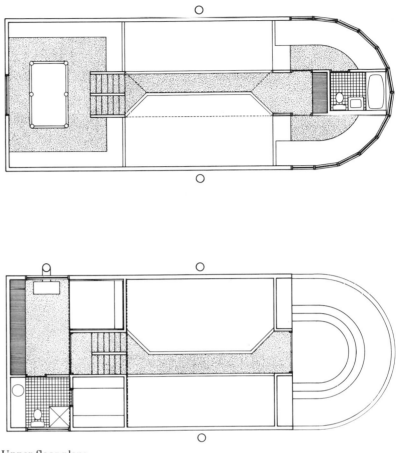

Upper floor plans

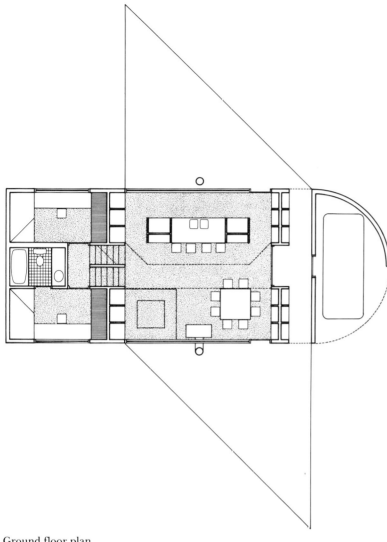

Ground floor plan

bility of man to establish order in the face of time and chance." This description of fragmentation can be viewed as relating to the years following the deaths of literally all the heroes of Modern architecture, when there were no immediate replacements for them of either the father-figure or Zeitgeist mentality. I reacted by developing, first in the individual projects discussed in this chapter and later in a more comprehensive way, the notion of argumentation itself—without any obligation to synthesize a new legitimacy.

The first time I implemented this notion was in a residential project designed for Oakbrook, Illinois, in 1976–77, where I ruptured a perfectly innocent Modernist stucco and glass house, revealing, as it were, its innards. The concept of shear as seen here owes a debt to another project I was working on at the time, The Little House in the Clouds (dealt with in Chapter 9). In fact, many of the projects from this point on will be seen to be based on my growing dissatisfaction with architecture designed in the tradition of "the spirit of all the ages" and not that of the new age, in which disillusionment with America's rather naive way of looking at itself had set in.

Around the time the Oakbrook project was evolving, I worked on another large residential project in Barrington

Metal and Glass House, Glencoe, Illinois, 1974–75

Assisted by Anthony F. Saifuku

An uneasy merging of the well-known machine esthetic with off-the-shelf components, this all-computerized house hoses down unwelcome guests who do not properly identify themselves. Programmed to have a remote-controlled robot laundry cart moving along a prescribed radio-monitored path, the entire system de-programs with suburban voltage irregularity. Looking for all the world as though there had been a change in the zoning, this not-very-suburban house coyly winks back at Leo Marx's harrowing Machine-in-the-Garden imagery.

View featuring astronomy dome and electronic overhead doors

Exterior photo at lake side

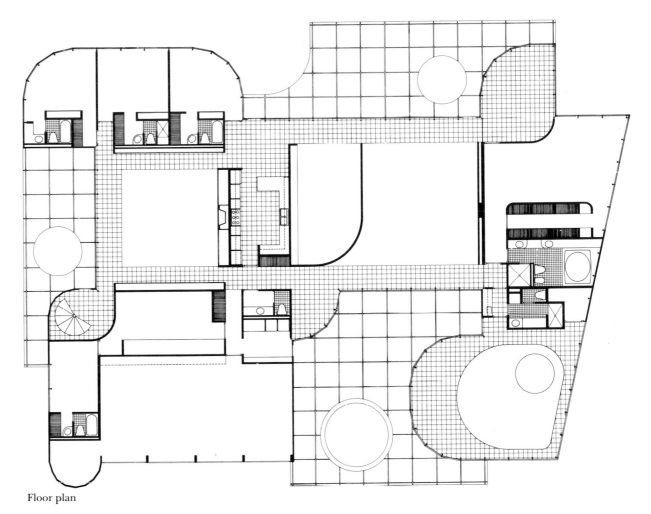

Floor plan

Exterior photo

Interior view of foyer looking through to swimming pool

Private Residence Project,
Oakbrook, Illinois, 1976–77

Assisted by David Woodhouse

A linear, curvilinear Modernist object is made more linear (or distended, if you like) by shearing the house into two parts and reinforcing that rupture by using stainless steel and glass. Whereas the building exterior is gridded glass and stucco-and-glass block, the rupture itself bleeds stainless steel. This project, while designed in the Modernist mode fashionable to the times, begins to dwell on the subject of duality as the pieces of the project are split apart and left apart.

View from artificial lake

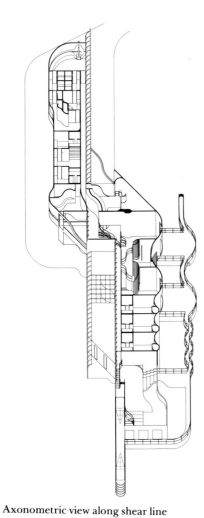

Axonometric view along shear line

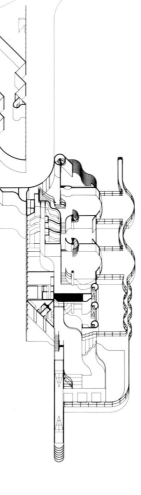

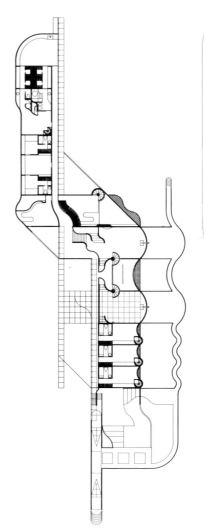

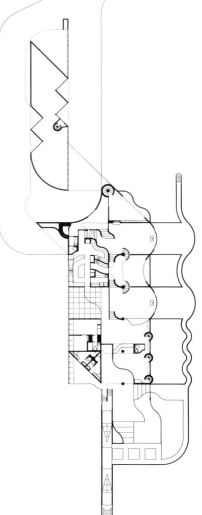

Floor plan

Model

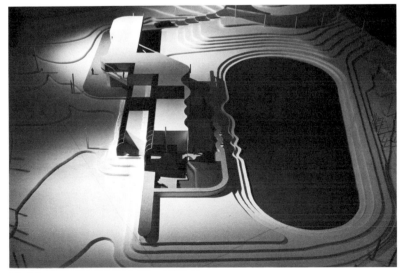

Model

Model

Private Residence Project,
Barrington Hills,
Illinois, 1976

Assisted by Robert Fugman
and Deborah Doyle

Main house, pool house and tennis court are separately disposed as three distinct objects in the forest. In furthering the notion of manipulating Modernist forms, each of the three objects has two distinct "faces": an uphill face that is opaque and curvilinearly reminiscent of earth contours and a downhill face that is gridded and mirrors the forest. A Magritte-like Stairway to Paradise penetrates each of the three forms, with cutouts of surrealist sirens out of the Homeric Odyssey, here signaling to each other in the forest.

Downhill model view

View from downhill side

Uphill model view

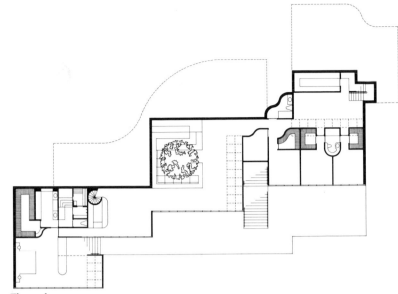
Floor plan

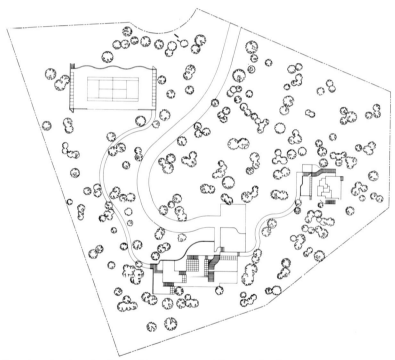
Site plan showing the three objects separated from each other

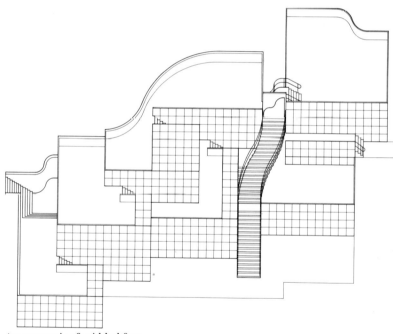
Axonometric of gridded face

Marion House, Lisle,
Illinois, 1978–79

Assisted by David Woodhouse
and Deborah Doyle

Here can be seen the notion of reversal (opacity vs. transparency,
public face vs. private face) and a
tortured distortion of the canoni-
cally Modernist binucleate plan,
deformed at its knuckle to feature
a Laurentian look-alike stair. Attempts to replicate the plan form
as fenestration are combined with
a strong hypotenuse to suggest in-
completion at every stage. Actually a suburban house in a builder's subdivision, the building's
materiality evolved from standard
American suburban construction
methods.

View of the public face

View of the private face

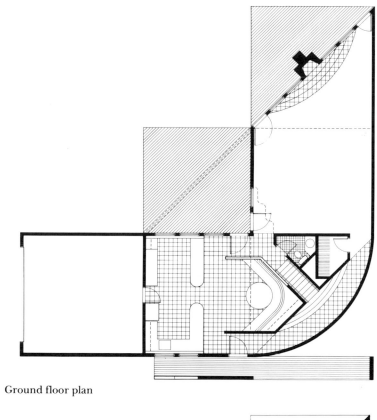

Ground floor plan

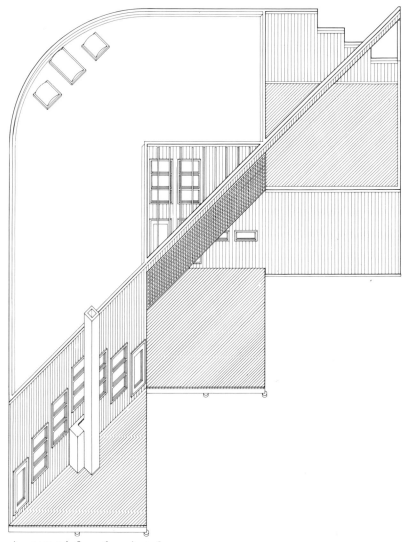

Axonometric from the private face

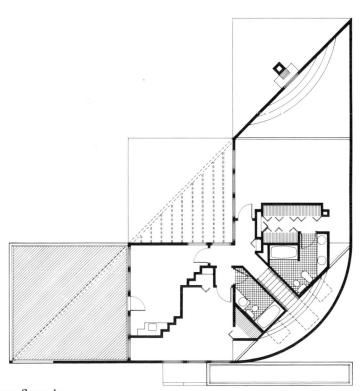

Upper floor plan

Detail view of the fireplace interior

Detail view of the fireplace exterior

Hills, Illinois, in which I embellished the concept of oppositions by treating the two sides of each of the three separate pieces of the project differently. In these two unbuilt projects I distorted conventional Modernist references in order to represent the dichotomous tendencies I felt were emerging in America during the 1970s.

By 1978 I had assimilated these feelings of disenchantment sufficiently to reinterpret them in a more inclusive manner in a house built in Lisle, Illinois. With this house I was able to express the concept of argumentation without resorting to synthesis either in the building as a whole or in its details. The building thus has a public face and a private face—the former opaque and the latter transparent. The traditional binucleate parti of canonical Modernism is here distorted and bent in such a way that the opaque public face wraps round one corner, contextually concealing the building's private face from the street and from a neighboring house.

Even though the projects in this category inevitably meld International-Style Modernism with Chicago-style Miesianism, they signal an end to my preoccupation with Platonic ideality. I now wanted to see both sides of a proposition. Inversions, reversals, ruptures, shears—i.e. oppositions—began to become apparent in my work, bringing to a conscious level the notion of the development of a dialectic.

Woodlawn Gardens, Chicago, Illinois, 1963–68. View looking west

Metal and Glass House, Glencoe, Illinois, 1974–75. View looking east featuring astronomy dome and electronic overhead doors

The Illinois Regional Library for the Blind and the Physically Handicapped, Chicago, Illinois, 1975–78. View of hypotenuse concrete facade looking southeast

Marion House, Lisle, Illinois, 1978–79. View of the public face at dusk looking south

House with a Pompadour, Ogden Dunes, Indiana, 1978–80. View of Lake Michigan facade at dusk

Animal Crackers, Highland Park, Illinois, 1976–78. View of entrance facade looking northwest

The Daisy House, Porter, Indiana, 1976–78. View of Lake Michigan facade

The BEST Home of All, The Museum of Modern Art, New York City, 1979. Aerial view of the American suburb

The BEST Home of All. View of entrance elevation

The Great American Cemetery, New York City, 1980–81. View of several cemetery plots

Bathroom Addition Project as Homage to Dante's *Inferno*, 1980. Axonometric looking upward toward heaven

Bathroom Addition Project. Axonometric looking downward toward hell

Bathroom Addition. Elevation

Private Residence, Kings Point, Long Island, New York, 1980–82. Elevation from Manhasset Bay

Private Residence, Kings Point. Aerial view of project at entrance loggia

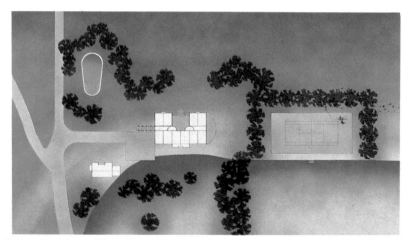

Private Residence, Kings Point. Site plan

Six: Surrealist Phase 1969–1979

A portion of this phase owes a primary debt to Louis I. Kahn, whose work in Bangladesh I was familiar with on a first-hand basis. The influences of Bertrand Goldberg, Hardy Holzman Pfeiffer Associates and, in particular, John Hejduk are found in this phase as well. Dissatisfaction among architects with canonical Modernism in the late 1960s and early 1970s resulted in many becoming involved with the exposition of structure—with mechanical, electrical and plumbing building techniques—as an "educational" rather than esthetic device (color coding comes to mind here). Highly colored ducting was one of the forces that ultimately led me to a kind of High-Tech design indebted to John Hejduk. Hejduk was in close touch with all of my work during this period and his work obviously had a great impact on mine—witness the similarity between his Barbar house and my Library for the Blind "window." Hardy Holzman Pfeiffer of New York City, Caudill, Rowlett, Scott of Houston and the later work of Metz Train Olson and Youngren of Chicago are examples of architects who operated with structural and mechanical exposition as the main basis of their buildings. My response to canonical Modernism was to investigate surrealist alternatives to the reductivist Modernist hermeticism.

The work in this style is oriented more to symbolic content than to formal and spatial manipulation, which characterizes the bulk of the work already discussed.

Monastic processional beneath drum-contained bell: Faith Bridge

St. Benedict's Abbey Church, Benet Lake, Wisconsin, 1969–73

Assisted by Anthony F. Saifuku

Benefiting from energy considerations (but not inspired by them), this earth-bermed, below-grade monastery church evolved through my admonishing the monks that if they hired a Jewish architect Christ would go "underground." The lozenge juxtaposition refers back to earlier paintings and sculptures of mine. The structure, the lighting and, most predominantly, the cross aisles reinforce the image of the crucifix such that the congregation, when queued up for communion, forms a cross, supporting the concept of the church is the people.

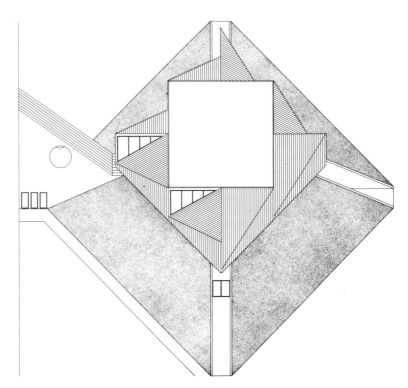

Clad axonometric expressing crown-of-thorns notion

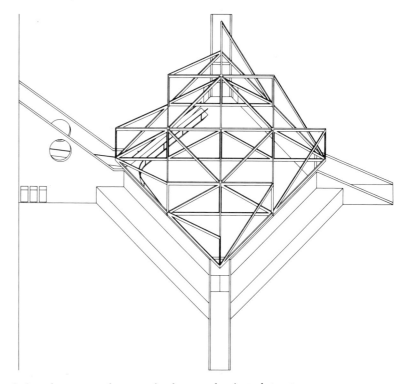

Stripped axonometric expressing lozenge dominated structure

View toward entrance

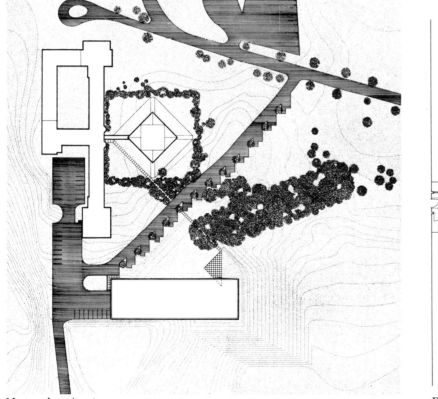

Master plan, site plan

Floor plan reflecting cross-axial communion reinforcement

Kelmer Arlington Industrial Building, Arlington Heights, Illinois, 1972–74

Assisted by Anthony F. Saifuku

Prairiebrook Commercial Mall, Palatine, Illinois, 1974–77 (opposite page)

Assisted by David Woodhouse

Both these projects show the obvious influence of Louis I. Kahn in the brick openings that are at once structurally rational and mystically appropriate. The industrial incubator is purposely denuded of scale crutches in order to render it as abstract as the original model form while the strip-center commercial mall is geared to captivating subliminally the mobile passerby. The earlier industrial Duck is contrasted with the later Decorated Shed as I move away from being a Chicago "waddler" and adapt the (now acceptable) Venturi fashion of the times. Note the suppression of the cheap Mies facade behind the masonry keyhole-screen wall on the strip center.

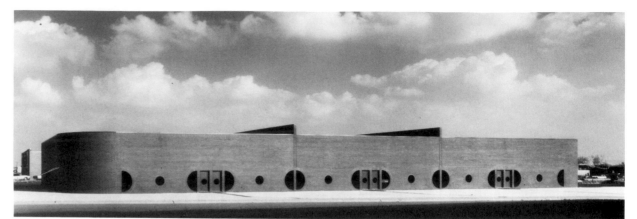

Incubator building pedestrian entrance

Incubator building truck-loading entrance

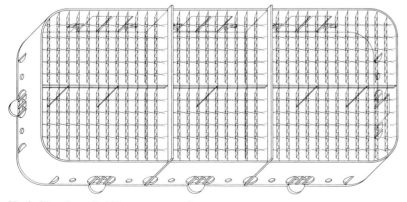

Unclad incubator building axonometric

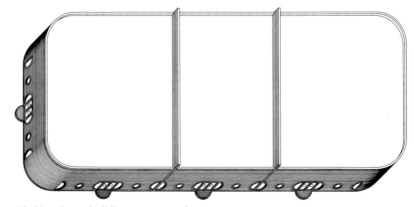

Clad incubator building axonometric

Strip-center facade

Detail along covered mall between keyhole facade and cheap Mies skin

The psychoanalyst Silvano Arieti has pointed out in his book *Creativity: The Magic Synthesis* that the coincidence of the rise of psychoanalysis and the birth of modern art in 1895—the year Sigmund Freud and Josef Breuer published their book on hysteria and Paul Cézanne had the first show in the world of modern art in Paris—caused a great shock wave in Europe. In announcing that he was not reproducing nature but representing it, Cézanne disregarded Hellenic esthetics and allowed a certain subjectivity to enter into his work. Arieti writes, "The influence of Plato, who gave prominence to the rational over the irrational and to the universal over the particular, started to be reversed....This did not mean that the rational and the universal would not be considered by the modern artist, but that the irrational and the particular would forcefully increase their participation in the artistic conception....First of all, it meant relying much more on imagery and imagination than on perception and memory; in the second place, it meant allowing the uniqueness of the subjective experience, whether originated inside or outside,

Frog Hollow, Berrien Springs,
Michigan, 1973–74

Assisted by Anthony F. Saifuku

A new life for a partially burned
barn. The blackness of the cladding, the arrow fenestration
pointing into the ground and the
end elevation simulating a
pumpkin face reflect the client
who (a) is a veterinarian, (b) has a
large pump organ and (c) keeps
white swans in the pond. Actually
a tightly budgeted barn remodeled into a house, its existing half-
timber structure was preserved,
the exterior and interior cladding
over insulation being the major
expenditures. It is an eerie sight in
the Michigan farmland, where
animals graze and people live in
the barn.

View of arrow window from pond

Exterior view

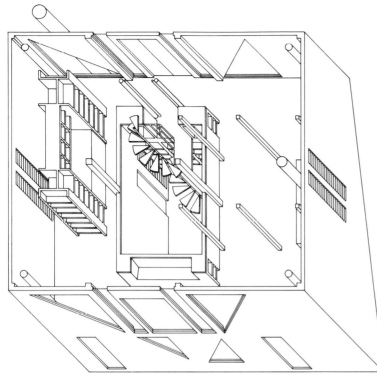

Axonometric 1

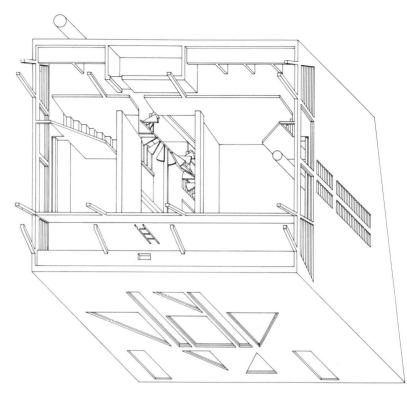

2

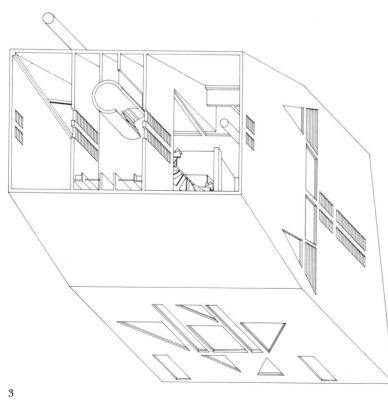

3

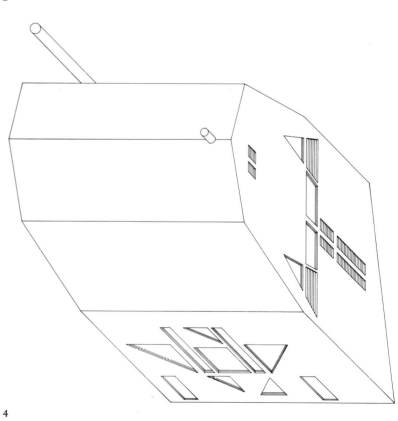

4

Hot Dog House, Harvard, Illinois, 1974–75

Assisted by Anthony F. Saifuku and Robert Nillson

Named from the plan form, this thin summer house is actually a study in reversals. It presents a blank opaque facade to the highway, from which it can only be seen at one point between a geometric grid of (now full-grown) apple trees. The opposite, or private, face opens onto an idyllic Walden Pond scene of "swimming hole," forest and crabgrass that in turn reflects back onto the neo-Mondrian (unnatural) facade. Thus an opaque but natural material (vertical cedar boards) is juxtaposed with a geometrically arrive-at grid of tree forms and this grid is opposed to a natural scene that in turn is juxtaposed with a transparent geometric facade. Exposed ducts, electrical conduits and raw wooden joists reinforce the rustic nature of this weekend retreat.

Axonometric from natural setting

Axonometric from highway

View of opaque facade (before orchard)

View from "swimming hole"

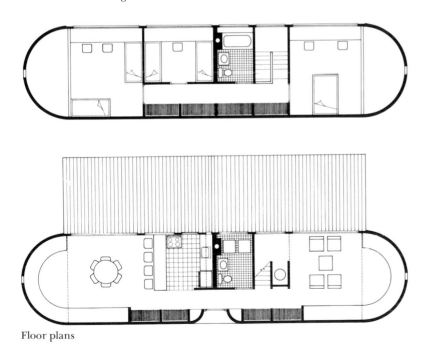
Floor plans

to be fully expressed. Thus different levels of the human spirit could now be shown at the same time."

André Breton, the founder of surrealism, Arieti goes on to say, "believed that absurdity is not just absurdity but an enrichment of reality—a 'super-sensing' of reality. The transfiguration of the dream, the delusion, the hallucination, are not deformations but an enrichment of life." Thus the beginnings of dualistic thought are found in the surrealist movement, in which double images abound (M. C. Escher, Salvador Dali, etc.). Arieti states that "the surrealistic school does not advocate an unusual matching of primary and secondary processes but an acceptance of both as they are, one beside the other. Reality and unreality would then be united to form a 'surreality,' an expanded universe."

The projects in this category were inspired by surrealism and by the clients themselves. As I moved away from canonical Modernism toward an involvement with the emotional content inherent in a specific architectural program, my work began to take greater risks. Though I was tied to functionalist programs, I wanted to enrich and elaborate on them by using the idiosyncratic element involved—the client.

Although both St. Benedict's Abbey Church and the Vollen Barn were plagued by earlier geometric preconceptions,

The Illinois Regional Library
for the Blind and the Physically
Handicapped, Chicago,
Illinois, 1975–78

Associate in charge:
Robert Fugman
Assisted by Richard Taransky,
Daniel Sutherland and Rafique
Islam in association with The City
Architect of the City of Chicago

A building for the handicapped
that tries to be far more than simply "barrier free," suggesting that
blind persons are as entitled to
metaphorical symbolism as are the
sighted. Tightly linear for the
purposes of tactile movement and
color coded (perimeter: red;
structure: yellow; mechanical
equipment: blue, etc.) because the
last thing a blind person can "see"
is bright color bathed in light, the
building has several metaphorical
inversions. The lightweight
metal-clad steel skin is opaque
while the dense concrete
hypotenuse wall is irrationally
broken by a Hejduk-influenced
(Barbar House) cut: all representing the irrationality connected
with blindness. Hard-surfaced to
encourage utilization of the blind
person's increased perception of
sound, the building has no hard
corners to maim and all objects
are anchored down so that their
position can be remembered.

View toward gateway

View of parking lot

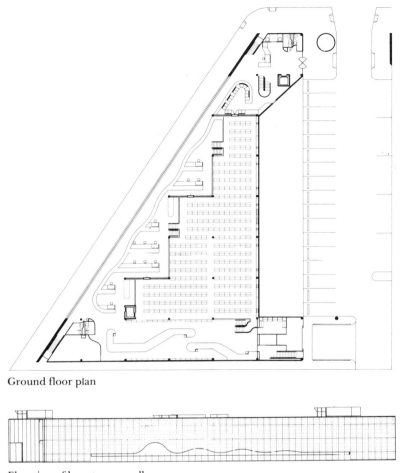

Ground floor plan

Elevation of hypotenuse wall

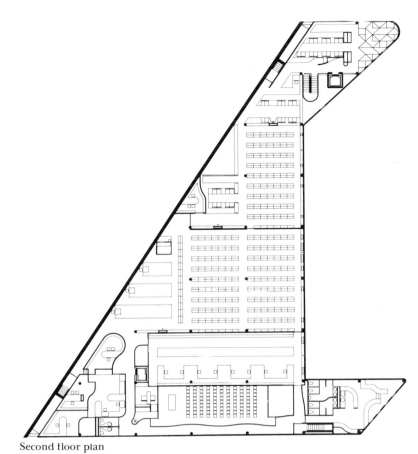

Second floor plan

they express my increasing concern (however veiled) with what the clients could bring to the project rather than with what I could bring to the clients. This very dichotomy lies at the root of the reversals and inversions and, finally, the schizophrenia that appear in my work. In the Vollen Barn, Frog Hollow and Arby's my use of coded color elements also shows a wish to communicate what a building is all about.

Concurrent with my desire to communicate through color was my interest in the poetic (albeit mystical) approach of Louis I. Kahn. Because of my own work in Bangladesh, I was directly influenced by Kahn's Capitol project there and it was only natural that certain of his forms would creep into my vocabulary. His influence can be seen, for example, in the Housing for Indigents, the Kelmer Arlington Industrial Building, the Piper's Alley Commercial Mall and the

Prairiebrook Commercial Mall Building. On a deeper level I was interested in another aspect of Kahn: his involvement with incompleteness and fragmentation. The Piranesi-like feeling of his interiors for the Capitol in Bangladesh seemed to me so refreshing. But it was Kahn's struggle with the polar opposites of his education and his epoch, and his inability to concretize his beliefs in fragmentation—about which he talked so poetically—that gave his work a poignancy I felt lacking in that of his colleagues.

My interest in struggles such as this culminated in my friendship with John Hejduk. His was the greatest influence on the projects of this time, for we conversed regularly from 1963 through 1978 and extensively criticized each other's work. My closeness to Hejduk led me from emphasizing color coding to concerning myself with the condition of the

Interior view of undulating patron counter

Interior view of undulating patron counter

Tigerman Takes a Bite Out of Keck, Highland Park, Illinois, 1977–78

Assisted by David Woodhouse

An idiosyncratic addition to an earlier house designed by George Fred Keck for the same owner, which reflects the resident's continuing formal bias. Hardly a study in contextualism, this new addition suggests that the two parts of the house are to be measured on their own merits. Actually a minuscule 500-square-foot addition over the master bedroom, it is an escape valve for the woman of the house, based on my response to the question: "What do you do for a suburban Jewish American Princess who has everything else?" You design an addition to give her the capability to escape from her family.

Exterior featuring reflective curved glass facade (the Machine in the Garden)

Interior

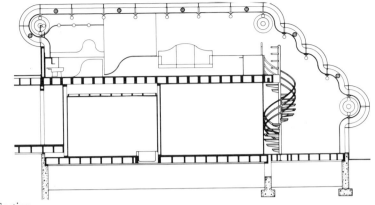

Section

Interior

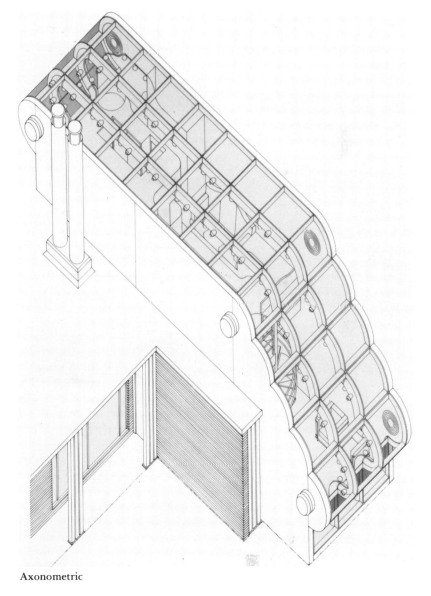

Axonometric

client, which, when interpreted by me, effectively became surreal. I perceived of the American barn in Frog Hollow, for example, as an isolated object in the landscape and dematerialized it by cladding it in one material (black asphalt shingles) of overwhelming, detail-less blackness. I also expressed my sense of the owner, a veterinarian who plays the organ and keeps white swans in a small lake adjacent to the barn. And I used the existing heavy-timbered structure to accommodate fenestration that, on the facade—in divining-rod fashion—points into the earth and, on the end-wall elevation, grins like the face of a Halloween pumpkin (dematerialized and spooky.)

Hejduk's influence is even more clearly seen in the Hot Dog House, a northwestern Illinois weekend retreat in which I created inversions of elements in such a way that natural forms (cedar boards) are related to a Cartesian grid of apple trees and a natural landscape is reflected in a neo-Mondrian facade—all of which is intended to invert surrealistically the reading of the object itself. But it is in the "wallness" of the project that it owes its greatest debt to Hejduk, in the oppositions intended metaphorically to suggest a past and a future, with the thin present the house itself: a concept that could not have come into existence without Hejduk's wall houses.

Much as I would like to think these buildings owe their organization and appearance to these formal concerns, they were actually influenced more by the nature of the individual client and by the particular context. My organization of a building like the Library for the Blind, for example, is based more on the affecting condition of the users, and on their entitlement to as much creative thinking as the sighted, than on the forms of Hejduk's Barbar House project, the source for the undulating form of the window in the concrete hypotenuse wall. Even so the stated "irrationality" of that window is an obvious allusion to the irrationality of blindness. Although the emphasis is on functionalism directed to the use of blind persons this is combined with surrealist attitudes dealing with inversion and reversal. The surrealist attitudes are used to communicate the sense of poignancy connected with the project on the one hand and an up-beat feeling—not without humor—for the benefit of the users on the other hand.

My underlying concept for Tigerman Takes a Bite Out of Keck was to make an addition to an existing house that would differ enough from the original to have an existence independent of it. I also wanted to substantiate my belief that a building can represent the particular time in which it is brought into being. Since this was a private, back-yard project, the importance of context was minimal.

Because of my concerns with reversals and inversions, and with inconsistencies I found in the client program, I became increasingly interested in the idea of struggle as a moving force in the design of buildings. In formal terms this struggle appears in my work in ambiguous Albers-like figure-ground reversals that have no need of resolution. But that aspect of the idea of struggle that interested me most was between the universal and the particular. In a deeper, religious sense, as the Jewish scholar Gershom Scholem has observed in his book *On the Kabbalah and its Symbolism,* "the principle is developed that the Torah is at once hidden and manifest, esoteric and exoteric….this dualism [is] not only in the Torah, but in every conceivable sphere of existence, beginning with God and embracing every realm and aspect of Creation."

In his book *The Sacred and the Profane* the philosopher Mircea Eliade sees the juxtaposition of opposites as anything but static. When he refers to the door of a church as a symbol of continuity he suggests that "the threshold is the limit, the boundary, the frontier that distinguishes and opposes two worlds—and at the same time the paradoxical place where those worlds communicate, where passage from the profane to the sacred world becomes possible."

The work of this phase represents the transition from an involvement with resolution and synthesis to one with incompleteness and fragmentation. As it reflects the changing values in America, the work begins to shift from the simplistic to the complex. When it attempts to transcend reality it approaches being ironic, and the issue of perpetuity versus the finite condition comes more clearly into focus.

Seven: Architecture of the Absurd 1976–1981

This is the first of my work to be influenced less by external forces than by dissatisfaction with my own earlier efforts at drawing, writing and building. I do not mean to suggest that antecedent figures ranging all the way from Claude-Nicolas Ledoux down to Hans Hollein were not influential in this phase, but their effect was peripheral to it. The mid-1970s in America were post-Viet Nam, post-Philip Roth and post-Woody Allen. It was America come-of-age in a time that was neither blindly patriotic nor fervently cynical but, rather—after its fall from grace—poignant. The work here is brassy, sassy and déclassé, and I suspect the reason why no other architects made moves in the same direction was because they considered it outside the mainstream of legitimate architecture. Bernard Tschumi in his article "Transgressions" in *Oppositions* 7 alludes to much of what underlies the work shown here. These projects deal with imperfection, death and irony, and I see them as peculiarly and specifically "American." The irony of perceiving polar positions simultaneously rather than assuming a traditional monotheistic posture is nothing if not American, post-Viet Nam style.

In his discussion of Kierkegaard's struggle to express the dichotomous state between the nature of God and the nature of life, William Hubben contends in his book *Dostoevsky, Kierkegaard, Nietzsche and Kafka* that religious references inevita-

The BEST Home of All,
The Museum of Modern Art,
New York City, 1979

Assisted by Michael Abbott, Susan
Regan, Kenneth Richmond and
Emily Patrick

Since WWII (an unbelievable 35 years ago!) the United States of America has quietly been nurturing a typological evolution as homespun as John Wayne—the suburban house. The objecthood of this form is as solidly American as Frank Lloyd Wright—embracing the hip roof (replete with overhangs) and the corner window and the wing-wall (both of which represent vestiges of Wright's breakup of the four-square, symmetrically axial, nineteenth-century aristocratic European box). Now the suburban house has an identity of scale as solidly real as the brick (Mies van der Rohe once said that "the brick is made to fit the hand"). By now, almost the entire recent generation-come-of-age has experienced the suburban context—the "Hilberseimer Tee-Plan"—brought into being in all of this continent's "Levittized" environments. Iconographically, the suburban house is as American as television (God knows, all of its aerials search-and-sweep the sky as so many centipedal antennae). Only one very small alien element clouds the otherwise clear azure dome over suburban America, the un-euphemized, un-cleansed, naked capitalist without any emperor's clothes at all, the commercial strip shopping center.

And so it was that the BEST search for a new home began. Really, they just had to find a comfortable place—one that could kind of nuzzle up to its little friends, so that when they came out to shop, it would be as if they never left home. If they drove to the store, why, they could just park their car right on the front lawn. The BEST mailbox would be just like their very own and it would only be four times as big. The garage door would be partially open just like their own broken one and the front door would be invitingly open as well, revealing an American-dream-come-true-at last...A 22'0" tall beckoning fair one as American and as wonderfully wholesome as Mary Tyler Moore. From the highway, their BEST new home would settle contextual arguments once and for all and you would never even really notice that each front step was 32" high, that the front door was 12'0" wide × 26'8" high, that the downspouts were 16" in diameter, that each brick was 15" high × 32" long (with 1½" mortar joints) and that you would walk right by the areaway-as-bench right into the basement window-as-door.

Nearly the BEST part of all was the four seasons. Halloween would feature a 10'0" black cat peering from behind the draped living room window with 10'0" hay boughs on the lawn and a grinning 8'0" Jack-o'-Lantern sitting right there on the front stoop. At Christmastime 16" lights would be strung around the picture window revealing a 25'0" Christmas tree and—on the roof—a 25'0" Santa, sleigh and reindeer. Easter would find 4'0" tall bunny-rabbits hopping up-and-down on the lawn searching for colorful 12" Easter eggs hidden between the cars. But the BEST season of all would be the Fourth of July. A 24'0" American flag would join the rest of the neighboring flags in celebrating America's birthday. Red-and-white striped bunting would surround the garage door and a 16'0" wide × 32'0" long × 10'0" high picnic table would be found at rest in the driveway with a 12'0" high Weber grill nearby.

Of course, the very BEST thing about their new home lay in its neighborliness insofar as they finally found an American symbol right there where they least expected it—at home in the suburban United States of America—and all of the snotty bastards in the urban United States were simply green with envy.

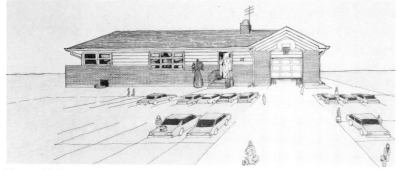
View at Halloween

View at Christmas

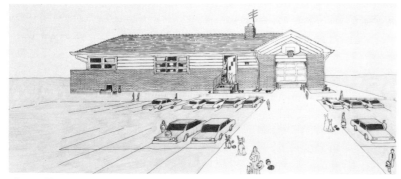
View at Easter

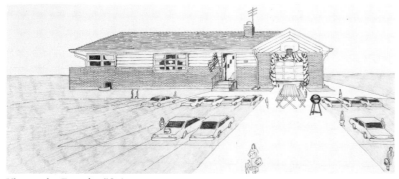
View at the Fourth of July

bly surface when the subject of humor is broached: "Irony functions somewhere between the aesthetic and the moral. Born of dissatisfaction and coldly critical of any imperfection, it remains egotistical and does not invite consent in spite of its possible truthfulness. But humor reveals understanding. It has a warm, forgiving, and sympathetic note and reconciles us with weakness or sin, whereas irony remains haughty and critical. There is, then, in humor the suggestion of a religious conscience, a sense of tragedy combined with the comic, and a promise of hope or reconciliation. But it may also contain a note of loneliness and even pain; it is frequently beyond communication and born from suffering; it thus prepares the religious stage in life."

The reason I wanted to incorporate irony and humor in my work was that I was unhappy with one of the conditions regarded in the profession as necessary to the practice of architecture: distance from the client. Until the mid-1970s I accepted this concept of detachment, which held that the ordinary and the mundane (the clients and their needs) should be separated from the perpetual and the ideal (the esthetic and the divine in architecture), and felt that a client's demands might interfere with what I had been trained professionally to handle: proportion, formal manipulation, structure, construction. But at the same time I became aware of the struggle in America in the late 1960s between egalitarianism and the issue of Viet Nam, which seemed to suggest that the mundane, even the profane, was a part of existence. Robert Venturi's book *Complexity and Contradiction in Architecture* was a passionate plea for an understanding of these issues, but it was a plea that fell on deaf ears—for the moment at least—as the powerful tradition of detachment prevailed. William Hubben quotes Kierkegaard: "To exist as a human being means to exist ethically and to face perpetually new moral choices. Aesthetic man remains detached and static, but ethical man is in the process of becoming. He evolves as a personality which combines the universal with his subjective being and thus partakes of eternity" (*Dostoevsky, Kierkegaard, Nietzsche and Kafka*).

The restructuring of American values, coinciding as it did with several specific events in my life, caused me to shift from the mainstream of architecture to an architecture interested in communicating with the American public, of which I was beginning to feel very much a part.

The Great American Cemetery,
New York City, 1980–81

In collaboration with
Richard Haas
Assisted by Michael Abbott and
Peter Hawrylewicz

As in much of the rest of American life, there seems to have been, at least up until now, a certain schizophrenic attitude about the American Cemetery. We wish to update the American attitude about death, and, for that matter, life, since we feel there is no longer any need for the American Cemetery to reminisce about earlier cultures. We now sense in an America that fell from grace and only then came of age, a maturation of ideals, both formal and ideological.

Just as America and Americans have for so long imported hi-art and good taste from Europe so as to gain legitimacy from their father, the American Cemetery has been the residual of the European sarcophagus, the aedicule and other remembrances of past cultures (Egyptian, Greek, Roman, Romanesque, Renaissance).

The art and architecture of a given epoch have always tended to mirror that epoch. In first-century Rome, for example, the buildings for the living as well as the permanent resting places for the dead were based upon the iconography, the decoration and the construction of the time. Now while America was in the process of coming of age there was every reason to import funerary art from the very place that the recent émigrés had come from. Thus, late nineteenth-century American art and architecture for the living were a necessary continuance of continental Europe. Artistic and ornamental models were combined with evolving American structural and constructional techniques as a comprehensive representation of the times.

None of this, however, was true of the American Cemetery, where objects resembling the Maison Carrée, the Nike Apteros and the cathedral at Rouen were thought to be sufficiently old to adequately represent a peaceful place of rest for those who had passed from life. Now, while it is true that avant garde forms have never been thought of as appropriate as an aedicule for the dead, the case can be made for communicating motifs of traditional quietude other than forms representing another time. Obviously, avant garde, modern or even contemporary formal reproductions suggesting perpetuity have not had sufficient time to gain enough legitimacy to represent timelessness. However, America has developed an entire range of forms within its existing residential typology that we find every bit as appropriate and as dignified for funerary monuments as the traditional Greek, Roman, etc., forms.

This residential typology has been evolving for the entire two centuries of the existence of the United States, and while it began as a necessary extension of the Europe the early American had departed from, it ultimately evolved into a set of forms that became so wholly American that its duplication into subtypes has reversed the trend of America's hi-culture importation. Levittown now exists not only in New Jersey but in Belgium and France as well. Thus, through repetitive usage, this funerary typology has, we feel, gained such a recognizable credibility that its transfer into "the little house" as funerary monument is appropriate.

Europe is dense and thus is represented by architecture and urban studies of like architectural appropriateness attacking the problems of density. America is sparse and the purpose of our project here is as a suggestion of the microscopic European émigré fleeing the density of that continent for the sparsity of this continent. The project can also be thought of as the single émigré fleeing from the collective morality supported by attitudes of "the good of the many" as that émigré flees toward the strength of the individual, that is, "the good of every single one of us." Therefore, our project may further be seen as the fleeing from the city toward the suburb as one moves through life back toward the soil from which we all sprang. Thus, our project is a box within a box.

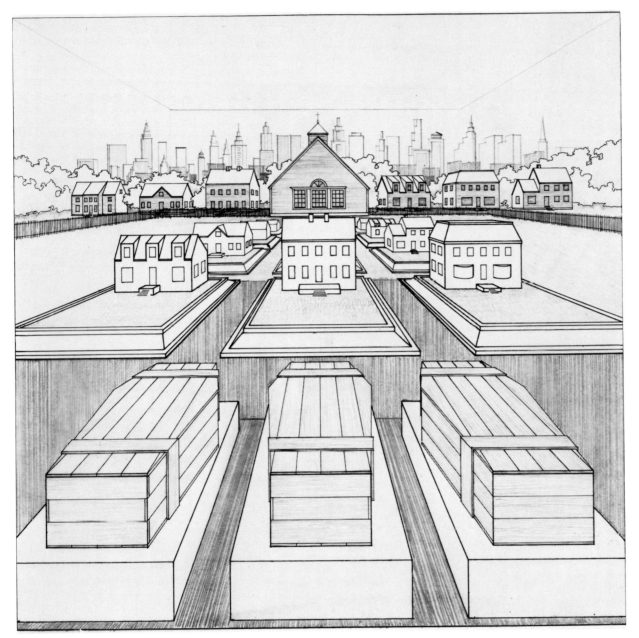

Perspective

The Daisy House, Porter, Indiana, 1976–78

Assisted by Timothy Sullivan and Daniel Sutherland
Structural engineer: Raymond Beebe
Mechanical engineer: Wallace Migdal & Drucker
Photography: Howard Kaplan

The house is a permanent residence for a family of four. It is sited high on a sand dune overlooking Lake Michigan, which is directly to the north of the property. The house is basically a binucleate parti with sleeping quarters disposed to the left and right, the adult quarters separated from those of two teenage daughters by the primary space itself. Informal family living is evoked by penetrating the house directly into the kitchen, which is located two feet above the living room. Access to the living room is made under a baldachinolike container that acts as a gateway.

The house, like the human body, is symmetrical on the outside and asymmetrical on the inside. Also the reversal of male and female is symbolized by the outside versus the inside. The house as a primary form is effectively three-sided and appended to the stucco wall, which in elevation reminisces about Spanish Mission architecture thereby effectively saying something about Spanish monks. That which is erotic in plan becomes a face in elevation.

It is structured by exposed wood joists laterally spanning the major twenty-foot spaces and has a cedar-scored plywood roof deck above: all of which is exposed. Peripheral walls (inside and out) are cedar-scored plywood, with the single exception of the north wall, which is stucco. All ducting is exposed and painted white. All electrical lighting tracks are exposed and polished chrome.

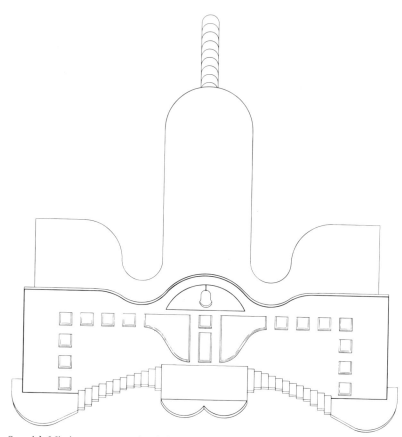

Spanish Mission axonometric winking and blinking at girls on beach

The first, though not necessarily the most central, event that occasioned this change was my contact in 1975 with the architects James Wines (SITE) of New York and Frank Gehry of Los Angeles. Both these men held attitudes about cultural attachments that were different from the attitudes of others in the building arts. Wines had already built renditions of his particular brand of irony for the Best Products Company—and I fell in love with them instantly. They seemed so apropos to the times, when our very existence in Viet Nam was, in itself, ironic. The projects' peeling and crumbling walls were a wry comment on the ruin of capitalist consumption and suggested that there was indeed a place for social commentary in architecture. My admiration for SITE and its projects for Best Products is reflected in my BEST Home of All of 1979 and Great American Cemetery of 1980. Frank Gehry's early Borromini-influenced, distorted-perspective projects for artists in which he captured the concept of pro-

cess in extremely fresh ways—and his unique southern Californian interpretation of life—affected the way I looked at architecture—and, for that matter, life.

The second event in my shift from the mainstream was my so-called mid-life crisis. Most Americans go through such a crisis and in my case it caused me to reevaluate the "seriousness" of life versus its "seriosity." Until 1975 I had always taken myself and my work overly seriously, but now, as I began to sense my own mortality, I felt the need to reassess the way I wished to live the rest of my life. I became fascinated with the idea that the notions of humor and irony could be regarded as perverse responses to the acknowledgment of death. These ingredients even now appear in my work though I have balanced the recipe to some degree with concerns about perpetual ideals.

Three projects that came into my office within a short time of each other constituted the third event. The first project

View toward entrance

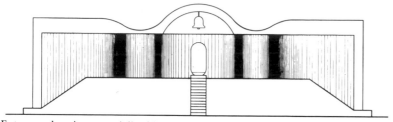

Entrance elevation materialized in vertical cedar boards

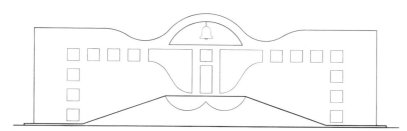

Spanish Mission side dematerialized in stucco reminiscent of Hejduk wall house

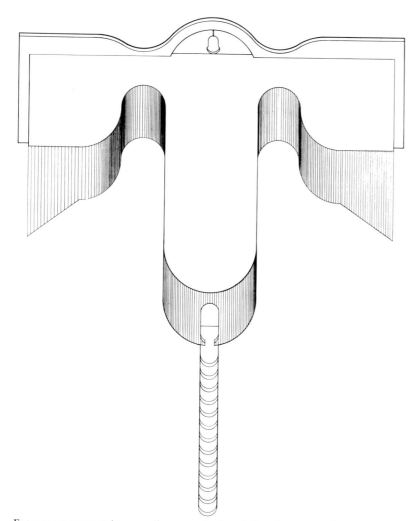

Entrance axonometric suggesting cause for low-flying planes to crash

was a library for the blind (discussed in Chapter 6), the second was a private residence for a man who told me he was terminally ill and the third was an addition to an Anti-Cruelty Society building. These three projects were concerned, literally, with blindness, death and sentimentality. With the poignancy that was already built into these three programs there was no need to overload or overlay them with extracurricular meanings. The necessity to communicate the finite condition of man in all its ironic nobility was an obvious requirement of each.

In the Daisy House, the house for the terminally ill—albeit exuberantly earthy—client I felt it was appropriate to make him laugh. Any metaphor that might bring joy to the project seemed important. Even so the selected metaphor of erect phallus, semen and scrotum was to some extent neutralized by the structuring of a Hejdukian wall house, with opposing sides dealing with materialization and dematerialization.

By extending the suggestion in the Daisy House of a building elevation as a face (or facade), the Animal Crackers project of 1976–78 uses biomorphic cues (windows as cheeks, door as nose, etc.) to structure a concept of entrance into a house that is otherwise simple and discreet. In its being symmetrical about one axis while layered about another, it has within it concerns about communication—body language, if you like. These biomorphic references are also at work in the Two-Car Garage project for the Illinois Regional Library for the Blind of 1977–78 and the House with a Pompadour of 1978–80.

Nowhere is the importance of the image more apparent, however, than in the Anti-Cruelty Society project of 1977–81. Here residential referentiality combines with anthropomorphic readings to create the image of an adoption, rather than euthanasia, center, as in the original buildings. The concept of a building as a sign, or a billboard, so to speak, is more than fully justified in this project. Here the positive notions of adoption—and of education about the attendant responsibilities—are expressed. The building communicates its message through historical devices such as the Palladian cutout, horizontal lapped siding and double-hung windows over a storefront and metaphorical devices such as the key to a can of dog food in the Palladian cutout, cheeks (windows) of a basset hound on either side of the entrance and tongue cutout in the entrance pavement.

Animal Crackers, Highland Park,
Illinois, 1976–78

Associate-in-charge:
Robert Fugman
Assisted by Wesley Goforth and
Gilbert Gorski
Interior design consultant:
Margaret I. McCurry
Structural engineer: Raymond
Beebe; mechanical engineer:
Wallace Migdal & Drucker
Photography: Ezra Stoller,
Howard Kaplan

As 2,500-square-foot house for a
family of three in the Chicago
suburb of Highland Park, its
major constraint was not programmatic but economic. Because
the assigned budget was extremely low the functional organization
had to fit into a minimum perimeter, i.e., a two-story housing-cube
with a one-story garage-cube appended to it. Using stucco and
wood—and exposed downspouts
and gutters and other items from
the genre of suburban home builders USA—the house alludes at
once to a calliope, a box of Animal
Crackers and even a Volkswagen
backed onto the property. The
primary intention was to establish
an image that would at once transcend the suburban genre and use
all the genre's components to
achieve that end. The house is on
a typical suburban site, which,
though slightly larger than the average lot (and, happily, wooded) is
nonetheless close to other equiva-
lently sized and budgeted houses.
It comments upon them as they
do upon it, and in a very real way
addresses the subject of an
economic suburban alternative.

Exterior

Ground floor plan

Second floor plan

Internal atrium

View into dining room

Two-Car Garage, The Illinois Regional Library for the Blind and the Physically Handicapped, Chicago, Illinois, 1977–78

Associate in charge:
Robert Fugman
Assisted by Wesley Goforth
Structural engineer:
Raymond Beebe
Photography: Howard Kaplan

Like the "big bank with the little bank inside," this two-car garage is intended to provide an upbeat attitude for a library whose users need as much optimism as possible brought into their lives.

Exterior

Exterior

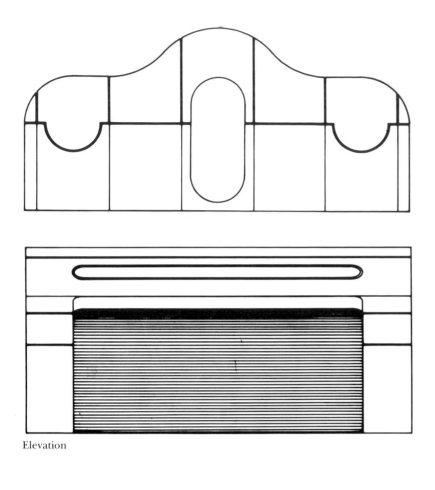

Elevation

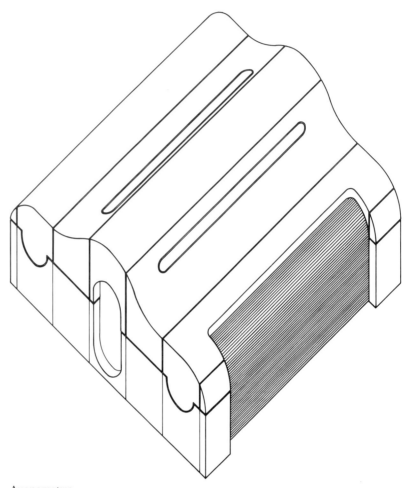

Axonometric

With these projects I was able to bring a modicum of joy into the lives not only of the clients but of the unsuspecting passersby. There is a great potential for this quality of joy in architecture, far greater than is suggested by the utilitarianism of Modernism. Antecedents for this approach are many, ranging from Claude-Nicolas Ledoux's unbuilt Maison de Plaisir to Charles Moore's Piazza d'Italia in New Orleans.

I think one of the major functions of a building should be to communicate an idea, story or fantasy. Buildings that interest me are those that can be understood by and participated in by all viewers. Unfortunately wit, humor and irony represent the illegitimate side of architecture and their use is often labeled infantile by serious architects. This attitude is symptomatic of Modernists as well as of Rationalists, who consider that architecture ought to reflect man's highest and noblest aspirations toward perfection and his belief that there is life after death. I believe, however, in the finite condition of man. I do not believe in life after death. A person's interaction with society is limited to that person's lifetime. An open expression of the imperfect human condition would thus represent the dark side of life. I do not advocate the use of euphemisms for reality but I do advocate leaving behind good works. Since many recent buildings express this dualistic view, which, owing to the humanistic trends in contemporary architecture, is more widely accepted now, this would seem a propitious moment to attempt to develop this dichotomy into a cogent polemic.

The connection between wit, humor and irony and reli-

The Anti-Cruelty Society
Addition, Chicago, Illinois,
1977–81

Associate in charge:
Robert Fugman
Assisted by Wesley Goforth
Photography: Howard Kaplan

The building is a second-generation addition to a building designed in 1933 in Chicago-World's-Fair Moderne with an addition in 1953 done in International-Style Modern.

The original buildings tend to symbolize the more unpleasant aspects of the institution as a euthanasia center. The current administration's intention is to reeducate the public to become aware of its adoptive, as opposed to its euthanizing, role. The image of the new building therefore suggests noninstitutionality. Residential imagery is communicated by what are thought of as apartments over a store: the second floor of the addition is fenestrated by double-hung windows over storefront windows (the old "doggie in the window" trick). The building is clad in horizontal aluminum siding, prefinished cedar gray with white trim.

Exterior

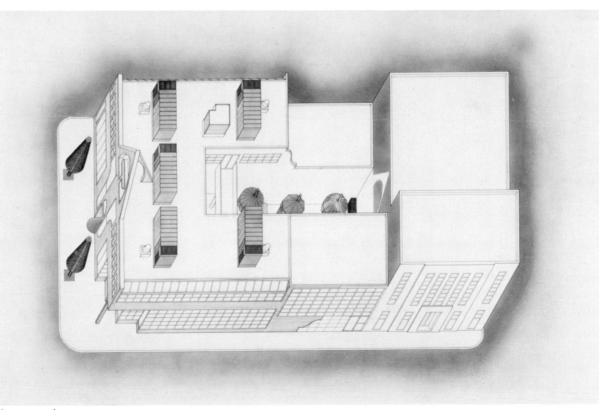

Axonometric

Elevation

Exterior

122 / The Anti-Cruelty Society

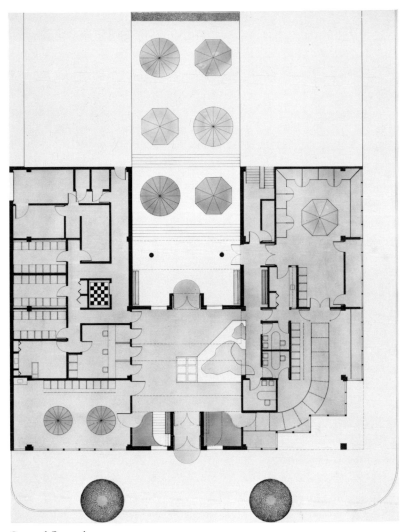

Ground floor plan

Interior view

gious beliefs has been recognized in the works of Freud and the essayist Arthur Koestler. In his book *Creativity: The Magic Synthesis* Silvano Arieti observes that wit has been studied often as a form of art, at times as a psychological process and occasionally as a special expression of the spirituality of man. In all events the expressions "sense in nonsense" and "clearness in confusion" deal with illuminations of truth.

By standing in opposition to known esthetic methods of expression, an Architecture of the Absurd can illuminate the truth. As black is best perceived in the presence of white, and the sacred in the presence of the profane, so Greek thought, which I see as spatial, should be perceived in contradistinction to Hebrew thought, which I see as temporal. William Hubben has pointed out in *Dostoevsky, Kierkegaard, Nietzsche and Kafka* that "the prohibition given to Adam not to eat from the forbidden tree produced in him this state of anxiety because he realized in the temptation the potential termination of his 'eternity.' It was sexuality that introduced the temporal

House with a Pompadour, Ogden Dunes, Indiana, 1978–80

Assisted by Robert Caddigan

A remodeling of a 1940s single-family residence at the south end of and abutting Lake Michigan, the project deals with the layering of images on an existing structure while fulfilling client programmatic imperatives.

Thus a pompadour (the client sports one) is set on the entrance elevation, which has a negative pediment and double-entry gates reinforcing the symmetrical penetration reminiscent of Palladio's Villa Maser near Asolo.

The lake facade now has the pediment, which has filtered through the building, solid, with its own cutout in the form of a reclining nude (the traditional symbolic siren luring those at sea)—all above a single central column that is thought of as a face.

Street facade

Street facade

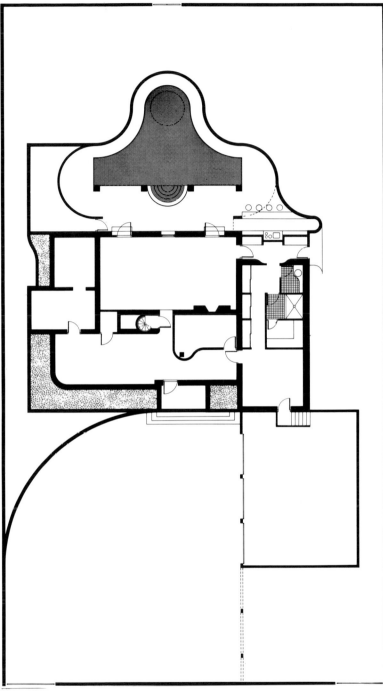

Floor plan

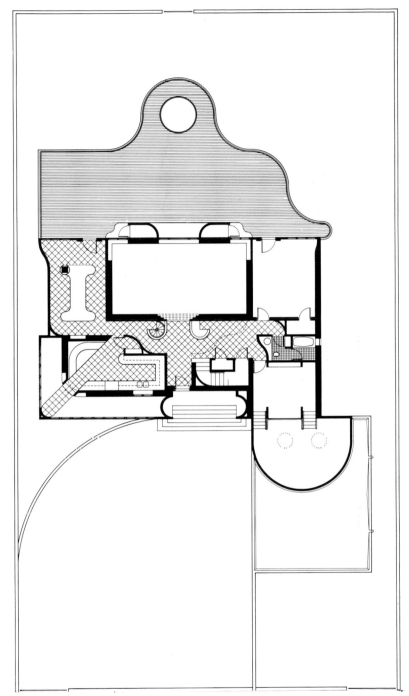

Floor plan

Street facade

Street facade (entrance detail)

into Adam's life. Existence, then, as a moral and spiritual state of suspense implies this 'thorn in the flesh.' Nearness to God can be experienced only in contrast to possible or actual alienation from Him. Only through extreme spiritual anguish can faith be won." The emotions of an epoch that wears its heart on its sleeve can be communicated back to it by architecture.

Eight: Historically Allusive Phase 1976–1981

The work in this group is concurrent with my Architecture-of-the-Absurd stage and shares with it my dissatisfaction with orthodox modern life. The work is almost (not quite) as self-energizing as the work in the ironic category. There is an obvious (and acknowledged) debt here to Michael Graves (his work) and Robert A. M. Stern (his knowledge) in areas of historical "revisitation." This category is possibly more Post-Modern than any of the others, assuming Post-Modernism to be at least partially Pre-Modernism in transparent mufti. As in the Absurd category, symmetry is used to relate to ideas about body language and the extrinsic (or story-telling) component of architecture to communicate with a wider audience than that of the architectural cognoscenti. Yet synthetically speaking, Modernist reductivist thinking (at least in plan) is still quite evident in my work (you never really get over your origins, I guess). In any case, the ideas and the work in this phase are less localized (Chicago/ Mies) than in the other phases and have more cultural and historical connections. This comes at a time when society in general—and America in particular—seems to be experiencing a kind of Orwellian awakening. As the debate between individualism and collectivism comes to the forefront of—and enlivens—the architecture of the 1980s, the controversy may not be resolved by my work in this category but it may at least be clarified.

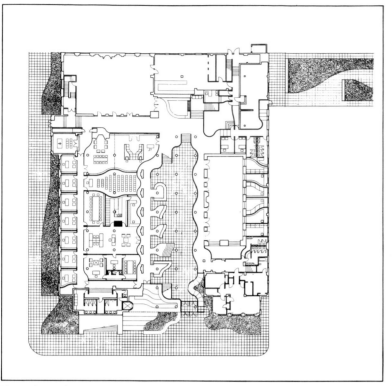

Upper level plan

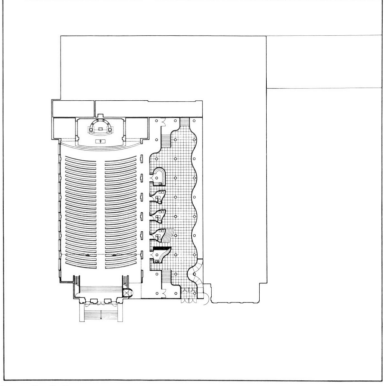

Lower level plan

The Cloud Room, St. John's Master Plan, University of Illinois at Champaign-Urbana, Illinois, 1976

Assisted by Timothy Sullivan, Robert Fugman, David Woodhouse and Daniel Sutherland

A master plan and addition to St. John's (the Catholic chapel at the University of Illinois at Champaign-Urbana, Illinois), the project's basic intention was to convey the notion of "memory through history." The idea is invoked by the memory of seeing columns punctuating the sky itself. When a column is seen without an architrave, entablature or roof, the image calls forth the idea of a ruin. Thus the Cloud Room has a trompe l'oeil ceiling and the original outdoor space is recaptured through memory. The programmatic nature of ecclesiastic functions further recalls the colorful processionals of a Roman hill town street—another reason for capturing outdoor space. Indeed the congregation and students form the "town" at each Mass, as priests wearing vestments and carrying banners proceed through the crowd in a linear liturgy. In this way queueing up for Mass takes place "out-of-doors," under the sky and beneath the clouds.

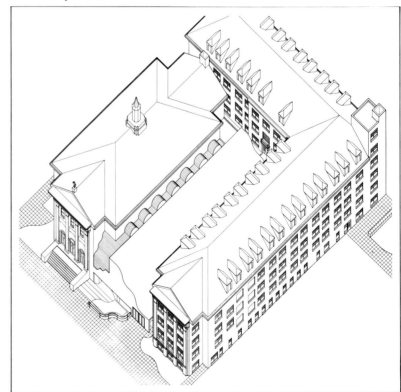

Completed addition axonometric

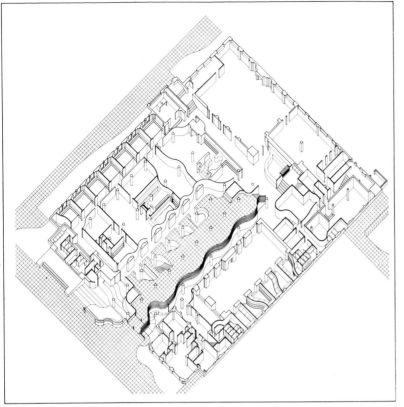

Lower level axonometric

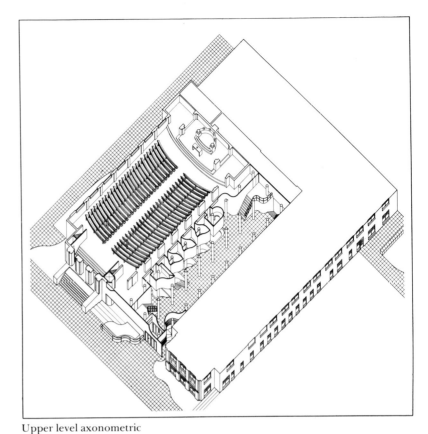

Upper level axonometric

During the 1970s a group of American architects frustrated with the unfulfilled promises of Utopian Modernism and bored with its minimal palette turned to the past in an effort to enrich their work. The most obvious source from which to borrow stylistic and symbolic fragments was the Hellenic Christian tradition, a tradition that has often been sought in times of stress such as those produced by the late 1960s in America. This direction proved too simplistic, however, and the architects soon looked to one that embraced the Judeo-Christian tradition.

What these architects found in the classical tradition—its decoration—was insufficient to represent or express the complex needs of a society in a period of agitated transition. My own work at this time was related to classical architecture mainly through its attempts to allude to the symbolic language of that tradition—i.e., symmetry, split symmetry, the orders, tripartite divisions—and to the spirit of the aedicule (in Sir John Summerson's sense) in which buildings reflect the human spirit as well as the human configuration. I was less interested in the totemic Platonic side of the classical tradition than I was in the side that celebrates human beings as frail, finite creatures.

The concept of communication is central to this body of work. Symmetry is used to split buildings into two identical halves, thereby suggesting biomorphic references. The two halves may remain apart physically but are optically rejoined by the observer. The idea is to push buildings into background positions. This concept developed in part as a reaction against the totemistic attitudes of Modernism that I felt forced buildings into unnaturally preemptive positions vis-à-vis people.

Poché was a buzz word in the late 1970s among architects. Like moving through layers of an archeological dig, "inhabiting the poché" meant thrusting into the insides of the walls of a building that was being split apart, as though leading back into cultural history.

Photo of model looking toward existing house

Photo of model looking toward existing garage

A Kosher Kitchen for a Jewish American Princess, Wilmette, Illinois, 1977–78

Assisted by David Woodhouse and Robert Fugman
Photography of model: Orlando Cabanban

The project is intended to simulate the American phenomenon of "cultural fulfillment." The site (the backyard of an existing neo-Mediterranean house in Wilmette) is subjected to a major kitchen/breakfast room addition conceived as an undulating topiary and butt-glazed wall that intersects the old building, but in a way that each retains its own integrity. A French garden (finely honed) is separated from an English garden (a vegetable garden) by an undulating walk that leads to the house from a garage storage addition and the alley. A point in the garden is selected as a kind of centroid off which pastoral scenes borrowed from Nicolas Poussin are painted in trompe l'oeil on garden walls and on the garage itself. A small pool is created out of the fantasy of inverting the negative spaces of the French windows of the existing garden room into topiary reversals, thereby thrusting the pool into mysterious semiseclusion.

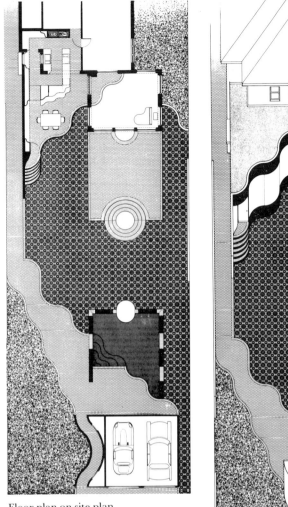

Floor plan on site plan

Axonometric looking toward
existing house

My own interests focused on split symmetry as a means of pulling a building apart in order to reveal its basic nature and communicate its purpose. I was fascinated by buildings of the past that were symmetrical about one axis and layered about another, in this way likening themselves to the human body. This use of the human metaphor in turn represented to me a sense of the ironic.

Another Pre- and Post-Modernist predilection that engaged my attention was the one for using fragments from the past. It was presumed the present no longer offered holistic ways of construction because of the general lack of artisanship resulting from egalitarian leanings (and trade unions). Venturi's decorated shed provided a means of utilizing a "fragment" as a concept rather than as a literal replication. Michael Graves has been a leader among those who have extended the fragmental concept that began with Venturi's decorated shed.

In 1976 a project for the Catholic church crystallized my ideas on the relationship between past and present architecture. The spiritual leader of the Catholic chapel at the University of Illinois at Champaign-Urbana commissioned me to develop a master plan to resolve certain spatial problems the institution had been plagued with for some time. The chapel required a vastly larger narthex than the one in existence, which would interface with the chapel and an adjoining dormitory that together formed two sides of a U-shaped complex enclosing a small, unused courtyard. My solution was to internalize the courtyard in such a way that it would stand in contradistinction to the existing dormitory and chapel. No attempt was made to match the earlier structures or even to approach the problem in contextual terms. A simple curving-roof structure was designed with a trompe l'oeil ceiling of clouds floating above columns—as if to suggest a ruin or a *rocaille*. No obvious or literal metaphors were employed but historical references are implied by the merest indication of columns bereft of entablature, pediment or roof.

From here it was but a short step to the Kosher Kitchen project of 1977–78 and the Highland Park remodeling and "greenhouse" addition of 1979–81. In these projects cultural, historical and stylistic cues were employed not to emulate the earlier buildings, or even to extend the context, but to create a dialogue with the existing Pre-Modernist residences. The Bathroom Project of 1980, in referring to Dante's *Inferno*,

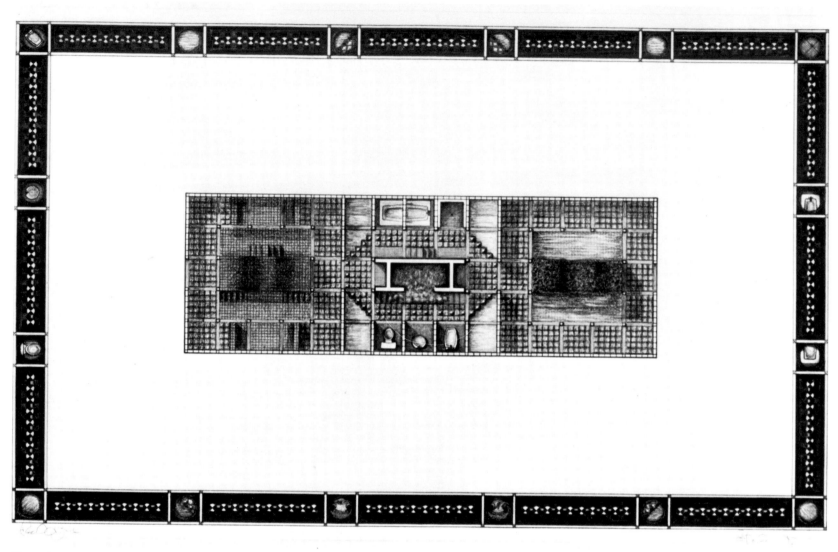

Floor plan

Bathroom Addition Project as Homage to Dante's *Inferno,* 1980

Assisted by Deborah Doyle and Patrick Burke

This project for the Kohler Company—intended for construction—is 5m × 5m × 3m high. It is entered one meter above the ground and is a total bathing environment unto itself, separated as it is from both the house and the garden. Heated independently, it has hot and cold plunges at either end. The entire structure is made of glass blocks with silicone joints where the walls are intended as Trombe solar elements.

Influenced by Dante's *Inferno,* the metaphor for purgatory is intended as absolution—the internal cleansing of the body. Furthermore water closet, lavatory, bidet, shower and tub reside independently of one another, each in its own altarlike space. The metaphor for hell is the steambath, into which one descends from the peripheral purgatorial edges of the little building. The heavenly metaphor is couched in a chaise longue, to which one ascends, with trompe l'oeil clouds painted on the ceiling above it.

The bathroom has suffered long enough from the excesses of Victorian privacy and this project intends to herald it as a place of joy.

Entrance elevation

A Private Residence in a Garden, Highland Park, Illinois, 1979–80

Associate in charge:
Robert Fugman
Assisted by Deborah Doyle, Polly Hawkins, Elizabeth Rack

This project for a family of five, with one in-house staff, returns to the humanistic values of the nineteenth century wherein life, not architecture, is celebrated. The house and garden are designed as poché pieces centering on the human being, the building being relegated to a background position.

Oriented to a southern exposure, all major glass areas are protected by overhangs based on the solstice. Windows are triple glazed and kept to a maximum of fifteen percent of the perimeter of the building. Long-span wood trusses bear on wood studs and the building is clad in stucco with a ceramic tile base to help with maintenance.

This project is significant for the recessiveness of the building, the topiary-cut landscaping and the use of symmetry to articulate entrance, receptivity and axiality.

Model

Model

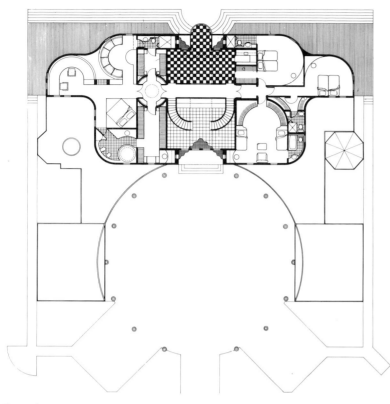

Floor plan

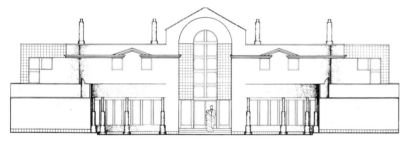

Entrance elevation

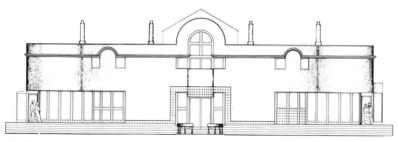

Garden elevation

Model

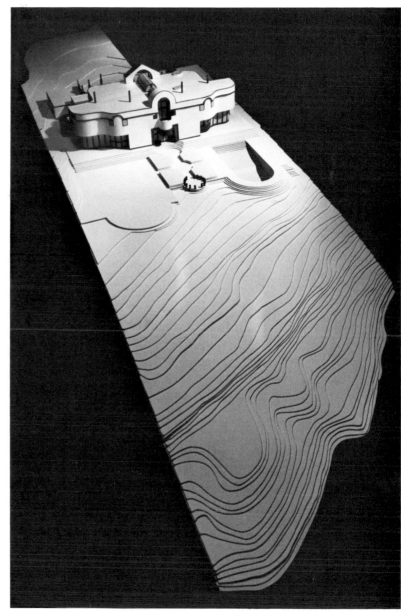

Model

Private Residence, Kings Point,
Long Island, New York, 1980–82

Associate in charge:
Robert Fugman
Assisted by George Hogan and
Andrew Koglin
Structural engineer:
Raymond Beebe
Mechanical and electrical
engineer: Wallace & Migdal
Photography of model:
Orlando Cabanan

The program is for a single-family house for an elegant widow, with facilities for her children and grandchild who are frequent guests. The site, which also includes a Queen Anne-style studio-guest building, is well located on a gently sloping plateau at the base of a hill overlooking Manhasset Bay. The client had for many years lived in a large Lutyensesque house and wished to retain some of the architectural biases of that building.

The solution features a primary axis of symmetrically disposed telescoped-gable elements that masks the real circulation system, which runs perpendicular to the primary axis. The major clue to the nature of the house is revealed in the fact that although each room is entered at a corner, the room is discovered to be symmetrical once one is inside.

Model

Model

Model

Model

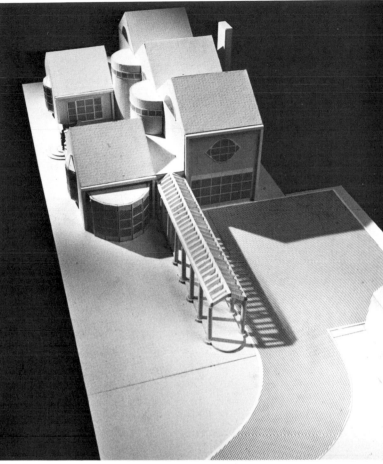

Model

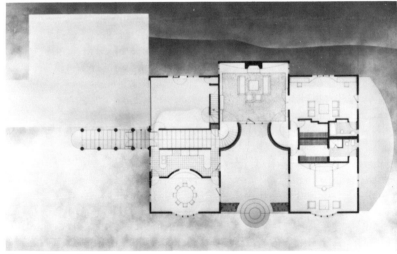

Ground floor plan

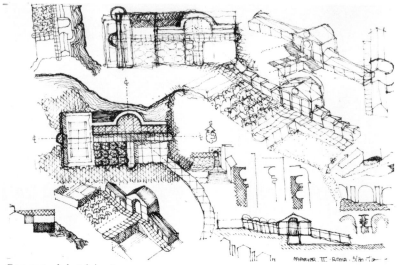

Conceptual sketch/cartoon

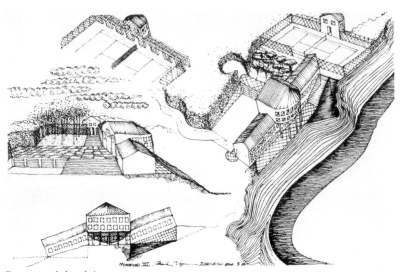

Conceptual sketch/cartoon

Elevation

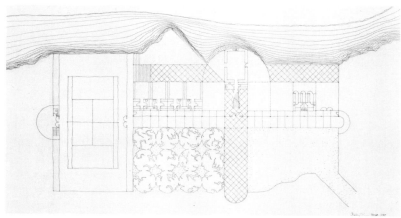

Floor plan on site plan

Private Residence Project, Crete, Illinois, 1980

The house is located on a large tract of forested land oriented toward the south and toward a creek. The creek is sufficiently downhill from the tableland to suggest that the house face in that direction. The program is for a family with four children with the requirements of a tennis court, swimming pool and guest house. The solution proposes breaking through the forest with an entrance road, which, at the parting of the forest, enters a courtyard whose top acts as a belvedere. The house is either entered informally at the garage, which has stairs rising up to the foyer, which, in turn, is axially related to the belvedere (actually the roof of the garage), or it is approached ceremonially on a long ramp leading up to a point of entry at the inboard side of the belvedere. Going on up that ramp one finds a terraced garden screening the tennis court. The tennis court is a continuation of the ceremonial entrance axis that ultimately leads to the guest building beyond the tennis court, ending this very long axis. The guest building itself is a diminution of the basic house but turned perpendicularly to it.

Various allusions at work in the development of this project are those to (1) Palladio's Villa Emo in the primary facade of the main-house, but here skewed, (2) the face at Bomarzo in the symmetrical facade of the guest building seen when looking up past the terraced garden and (3) Palladio's Basilica in Vicenza (modestly) in the faces used as column capitals that in turn are trabeated with triumphal arches. But the transformative qualities of skewed building and secret garden sufficiently mask any direct allusions to such an extent that a new synthesis is, I believe, created.

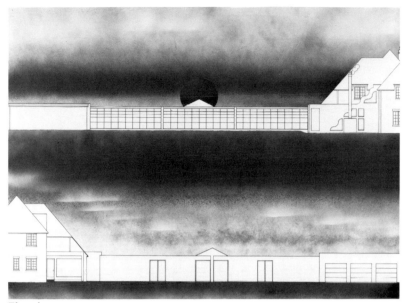

Elevation

Elevation

Remodeling with Addition to Private Residence, Highland Park, Illinois, 1979–81

Associate in charge:
Michael Abbott
Assisted by Andrew Koglin
Structural engineer:
Raymond Beebe
Mechanical and electrical engineer: Wallace & Migdal
Photography of model:
Orlando Cabanban

The program was to remodel an existing kitchen and garage into family-kitchen facilities and to design a greenhouse and a new three-car garage for a family of three.

The solution reflects an interest in the juxtaposition of disparate elements (existing house and new construction) without resorting to Hegelian synthesis. The struggle here is between the original design for Client A and the new design for Client B, the juxtaposition thus suggesting a dialectic.

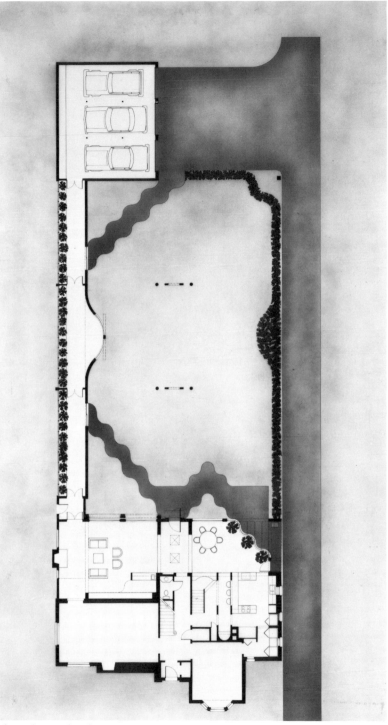

Floor plan on site plan

also attempts a dialogue—but with literature, not with architecture.

The "garden villa" in Highland Park of 1979–80 was my clearest attempt to delve into the split-symmetrical world in which the building is removed from center stage and placed as backdrop. The building and landscaping here were conceived as topiaries embracing man, the central figure. Allusions to the Villa Madama by Raphael and Giulio Romano and the Villa Giulia by Giacomo da Vignola in Rome add to the historic referentiality. Quoting earlier architects was a device frequently used during the latter part of the 1970s by architects such as Allan Greenberg and Robert A. M. Stern.

My most obvious moves in this direction were in the invoking of Sir Edwin Lutyens in the Kings Point, Long Island house of 1980–82 and of Andrea Palladio in the unbuilt residential project in Crete, Illinois of 1980. These projects also gave me the opportunity to develop a dialectic within the formal organization of each. The basic organization of the Kings Point house demonstrates the Lutyensesque concept of having the entrance represented not by the major axis of symmetry but by the minor axis—in this case the telescoped gables. This was my somewhat perverse way of suggesting opposites at work in the formal organization of the house. Alluding to the Hellenic tradition of spatiality wherein the whole space is seen from different points of view, each room in the house is entered at a corner. When the rooms are separated from the whole, however, each is found to be locally symmetrical. In the residential project in Crete references are made to the Renaissance garden at Bomarzo and Palladio's Villa Emo at Fanzolo, although these visions are distorted by the building's being tilted, as if dislodged by a seismic shift. Thus a belvedere is created with a monumental axis that cannot be used for the processionals it implies.

These projects reflect my uneasiness with the Hellenic tradition of secular thought, whose beginnings date back to five centuries before Christ. Within this tradition explanations were sought for things hitherto left to the realm of myth. It was the start of mankind's effort to come to grips with the universe—the inception of pure reasoning. In the process of questioning the "irrational," or mythic, the Hellenic mind divided everything into two opposing parts—objectivity and universality on the one hand and subjectivity and relativity on the other. These two opposing concepts gnawed at my sensibilities, and I struggled with the outrageous possibility that architecture could represent both simultaneously. The notion of two worlds, which Plato himself confronted, was at the source of my emerging consciousness. One world was unseen and ephemeral, ideal in form and having perpetual values presided over by God, while the other was an imperfect, materialistic replica of that same world—life itself. Plato's reconciliation of these opposites nonetheless took nothing away from the dichotomy that was central to Christian theology, which also had its origin in the Jewish dialectic. Between the idea and the object, when synthesized and made divine by Plato, was also the fact of the split between Plato and his student Aristotle.

The Little House in the Clouds, 1976. Aerial view of model

One of the primary concerns has been to order the site, and therefore to create a new wholeness and completeness to the complex. This has been achieved primarily through the use of symmetry which incorporates the existing buildings. These buildings now contain new meaning and value with the centerpiece and focus of this revamped complex being the new adminstration building.

The administration building is a perfect cube of 29 meters, sitting on a plinth, which is placed within a square, surrounded by stainless steel pergolas. The building is rotated about the orthogonal grid of the rest of the site in order to distinguish it from the existing buildings and to symbolize the separation of production and administration. It is clad in a grid of polished pink granite and pink mirrored glass. The strong gridding makes it scaleless, and only the windows, barely visible during the day, give away the position of the floors. The grid is carried from the building, down the plinth, to the surrounding pavement thereby linking it to the ground and thus symbolically to the outside world. On the plinth, the windows continue, becoming lights which, at night, illuminate the building and the pavement. This, in a separate manner, disconnects the building from the ground and creates an ambiguity and tension in the design.

The edges of the plinth are wrapped by the granite-paved roadway and pergola which continue along the major east-west axis in both directions. To the west, this arena, facing the direction in which visitors will arrive and consisting of the five sales divisions, the reception hall, and product presentation. The north half of the building, facing the factory, is the private arena of accounting, computing, designing, directing, and training. (285 square meters/floor net area, 360 square meters/floor gross area; 3420 square meters total net area, 4320 square meters total gross area). Thus the building is split between those who represent the company and interact with the outside world, and those who technically and managerially operate the company.

In the center of the building is the circulation zone, with two scissor stairs and toilets on each side. Two elevators link the halves. The elevators become the sign for the building, traveling up and down and highlighting the essential intricacy and movement of the D.O.M. product. The movement from one half of the building to the other through the elevator, from the public side to the private side, becomes highly symbolic in that the elevator in itself becomes a security lock. It also stresses the ambiguity and obscurity of whether the building is one or two buildings: From afar the building is a cube, but as one approaches it, the building splits in two.

The building is constructed on a nine square concrete column and waffle slab grid which aligns with the grid of the pergola. Over the span of 9.6 meters the waffle slab is structurally logical, hiding services and lighting, providing lines for partitions on a regular grid creates the main entrance to the building and to the east, a vista from the autobahn. Under the pergola in this east-west direction lies water, emphasizing the line of the rising and setting sun. The water beneath the trailing plants and vegetation provides a stillness and restfulness to the landscape in contrast to the rigidity of the buildings.

Along the entire length of the axis is a 4.2 meter wide cut of a golden yellow color which slices through both the pergola and the building showing that something more than human is involved in the workings of mankind. The inside of the building is now revealed through clear glass and the sensuousness of the interior workings are unmasked, for it is as an anonymous mask that the building normally presents itself to the world. The interior workings reveal a complexity in a way which is not normally seen. The building is, in fact, a tripartite building with firstly, the two story entrance hall, secondly, the five floors of offices, and thirdly, the roof garden. This also indicates the coding of the building with ascension from the ground and market place, up through the building (the senior employees and greater sumptuousness being nearer the top) to the heavenly garden, where employees can reflect and contemplate on the position of themselves, the company, and the world. The pergola and water are carried through on the roof of the building to connect heaven with earth.

The functions of the building are split in two, quite naturally, by the program. The south half is the public and thereby creating flexible office space.

The service entrance to the building is from the east with direct access to the kitchen, storage space under the exhibition area, and a basement which houses the mechanical plant. The garaging for the executive cars is to the west of the building and acts as an entrance front to the square on which the building sits. A colonnaded walkway runs along the west side of this garage. The main employee and service vehicle entrance is to the north along the lines of the original entrance. The two existing chimneys are repeated on the other side of the major axis by two flagpoles of exactly the same form and material with the D.O.M. and West German flags.

To the north and the south of the site are two banks of trees which provide a natural barrier against the adjacent industrial areas. The trees are conceived as topiaries and take on the shape and size of the buildings they mirror. To the north they reflect the main factory building and indicate the area for future expansion. To the south they reflect the outline of the south side of the existing complex and create a vista and square in the Renaissance tradition. This tree/building situation acts as a dialogue between the man-made and the natural, with the natural under the control of man. The headquarters is now seen as a precise, elegant, and succinct form sitting in an ordered environment of water, trees, grass, and buildings.

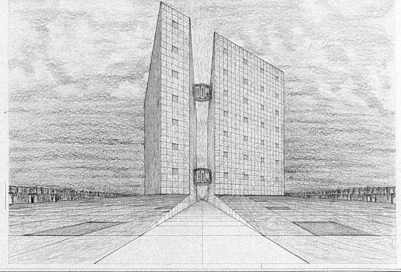

D.O.M. Competition Corporate Headquarters Project, Bruehl (Cologne), West Germany, 1980. Elevations.

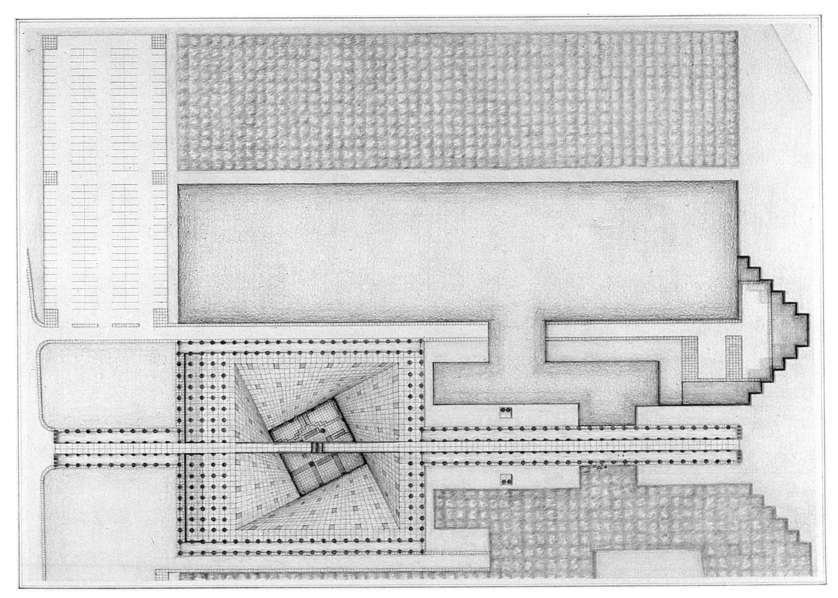

D.O.M. Competition. Site plan.

Exhibition, Thonet Showroom, The Merchandise Mart, Chicago, Illinois, 1981. View looking toward the unresolved dialectic

Nine: Post-Modernism is a Jewish Movement 1976–1981

It must be understood that the cosmicization of unknown territories is always a consecration; to organize a space is to repeat the paradigmatic work of the gods.

Mircea Eliade, *The Sacred and the Profane*

Anthropology is theorized and taught as an effort to rationalize *contradiction, paradox and dialectic.*

Roy Wagner, *The Invention of Culture*

Showing that it is possible to develop a case for a dialectic without having to revert to Hegelian methods of synthesis, the projects in this chapter embellish this dialectical concept in formal, spatial and programmatic ways. They invite the observer to reassemble visually their broken or ruptured parts at the same time as they posit the troubling notion that with no one there to do the reassembling these same parts lie in disarray. The question comes to mind: When a tree falls in the forest with no one present, does it make a sound? Since Platonic form is complete in and of itself, requiring no additional perceptual involvement, the kind of architecture that does require participation needs explanation.

In the Platonic tradition buildings are conceived as representing eternal—as well as contemporary—civilization and divine qualities are quantified by which the buildings can be measured. This formal tradition has been in opposition to

The Little House in the Clouds, 1976

Photography of models:
Orlando Cabanban

This is the story of the primeval house standing under the stars. The house has sacred pillars with Corinthian capitals that support a celestial soffit of clouds suggesting a heavenly trompe l'oeil.

We look back to the beginning of man in opposition to nature. Primal man sees in his mirror image a voyeur trapped in history. The land inflects as if depressed by the weight of the foreign objects placed upon it. The downward deformation embraces both the house and the trees which are halved with scalpel-like precision. One half of the house returns to nature while the other half becomes man's vestigial home.

The house on pilotis and its topiary mirror image across the Yellow Brick Road suggest a ritualistic dance. The earth recedes, removing itself from what might become a struggle or an embrace.

Far into the future as sentinels they stand…and watch… and wait.

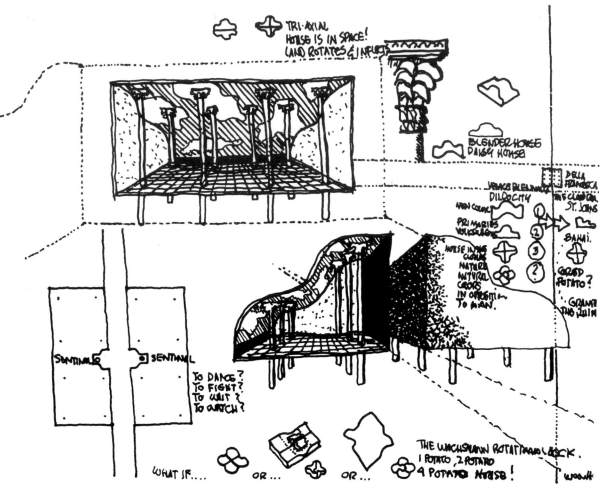

Drawing/cartoon

the rational throughout history, the two alternating with each other as each exhausts its technological and symbolic potentials. When neoclassicism declined after the Renaissance with the lessening of interest in Greco-Roman archeological forms, formalism was thus replaced by the rationalism of the neo-Gothic as expounded by Viollet-le-Duc and John Ruskin. When the rationalism of the neo-Gothic in turn died due to its limited palette, it was supplanted by the formalism of Victorian decoration. When this throwback to decoration had run its course, it was superseded by Modernism in the early twentieth century. This time, however, rational thought ran parallel with an international social revolution that provided justification for its avant-garde polemics.

I propose to demonstrate that formalism and rationalism can coexist and, in addition, that they can reinforce each other when set in opposition (black is best seen in the presence of white). Traditional methods of synthesis always involve a winning and a losing side. My goal is to reject synthesis and attempt through argumentation to elaborate, embellish and enrich each side alternatively. Each side of the architectural argument has not only a separate entity but an incomplete one (through rupture, shear, etc.), requiring the viewer to participate in the physical dialectic in order to understand—indeed to complete—the project.

When architecture and its divine measuring capability moved toward Platonic thought during the Renaissance, the sense of the perpetual and the ideal in Western architecture was codified. This codification was what American architects

Model

Model

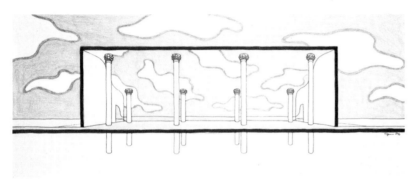

Drawing/cartoon

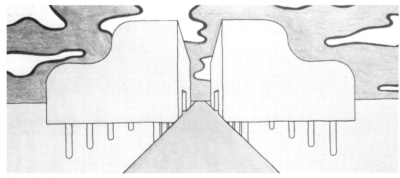

Drawing/cartoon

sought in the late 1970s as a panacea in turbulent times. For the first time in architectural history, however, the simplistic solution of replacing one approach with its opposite proved to be unsatisfactory. The complexities of a sophisticated yet essentially ruptured culture demanded a more comprehensive response than that provided by pure Platonic thought. If Plato saw his two worlds—this one and the next—as stemming from reason, and Christianity saw these same two worlds as proceeding from revelation, then architecture would serve both.

The historicism that became the crutch of Post-Modernism dredged up values common to the Hellenic-Christian tradition. But just below the surface of this Hellenic-Christian tradition lurked the Aristotelian concept of unsynthesized dialectic, with its almost equally long, though not nearly as lustrous, tradition. The Aristotelian tradition was resurrected by a Christian, a Moslem and a Jew—St. Thomas Aquinas, Averroës and Maimonides—in the twelfth and thirteenth centuries. Relegated to the shadows in the Renaissance, Aristotle's dualism since then has remained sufficiently in evidence to gather its own complex legitimacy. This is what is now once more working its way free—to be utilized by a society complex enough to comprehend fully that dialectic.

Perhaps the most fascinating approach philosophers have made to the study of "contradictions" between Hellenic and Hebraic attitudes is the one that involves attempts to translate dualistic thought into physical form. In his book *Hebrew*

Baha'i Archives Center for the National Spiritual Assembly of the Baha'i Faith of the United States, Wilmette, Illinois, 1976–82

Renderings by Mericke Phillips
Associate in charge:
Timothy Sullivan
Assistant: Wesley Goforth
Structural engineer:
Raymond Beebe
Mechanical engineer:
Ted Skrzenta
Electrical engineer: Don Ramey
Photography of model:
Orlando Cabanban

An element of timelessness is involved in this project insofar as the client wished to evoke a thousand-year-old building. In order to achieve this end, a square was bisected. Half of the square reverts to nature in a mirror-image topiary of the other half, which becomes man's perpetual home. It is the story of the Celestial Soffit in which the sacred pillar as tree trunk supports real leaves with real clouds and sky over all. The sacred pillar is also thought of as a column supporting the acanthus leaves of a Corinthian capital, with the sky a trompe l'oeil painted on the underside of the roof. Functional elements within the structure have their own roofs and are like small buildings in a village. There is no detail. Everything is dematerialized, supporting the contention of timelessness while eradicating the feeling of now. The overall square is on axis with one of the nine sides of the temple, but the structures on it are hidden from the temple by a great earth form. The occasional visitor will conclude that nothing has changed. The Baha'i Temple continues to predominate.

Model

Model

Thought Compared with Greek, Thorleif Boman writes, "If Israelite thinking is to be characterized, it is obvious first to call it dynamic, vigorous, passionate, and sometimes quite explosive in kind; correspondingly Greek thinking is static, peaceful, moderate, and harmonious in kind." In an article entitled "Zeit und Raum" in the *Journal of Biblical Literature,* E. von Dobschutz believes that the thinking of the Greeks is spatial and the Hebrews' temporal. Anders Nygren in his book *Agape and Eros* defines the difference between the Hebraic concept of love, agape, and the Platonic, eros, as: "Agape is the free and unmerited love that comes from God and flows toward man, and Eros is the love that stems from man and strives toward God."

The artists' struggle to identify opposing points of view in visual terms is interestingly documented by the art historian William Loerke in his article "Observations on the Representation of Doxa in the Mosaics of S. Maria Maggiore, Rome and St. Catherine's, Sinai" in *Gesta,* in which he discusses the problems Hellenic artists faced in depicting the scene of God making his presence known to man. That encounter (which

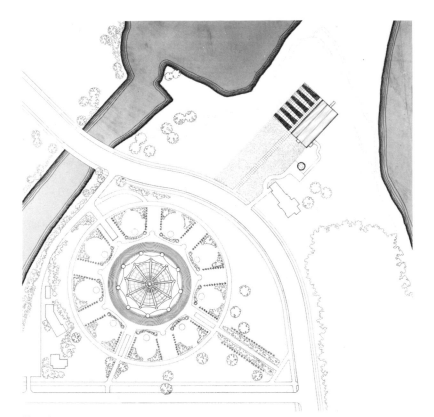

Site plan

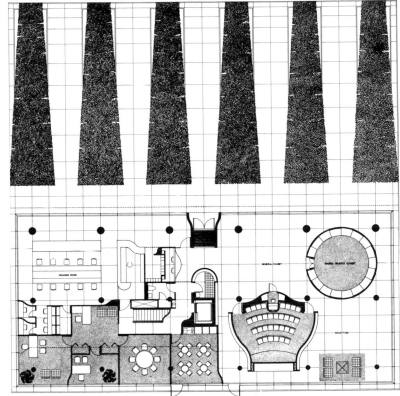

Floor plan

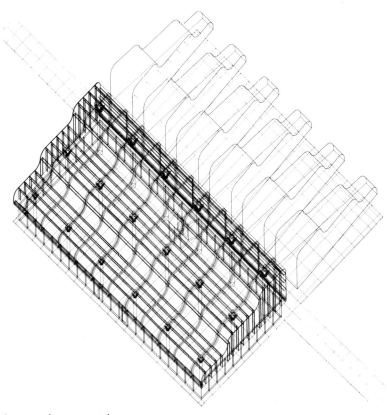

Structural axonometric

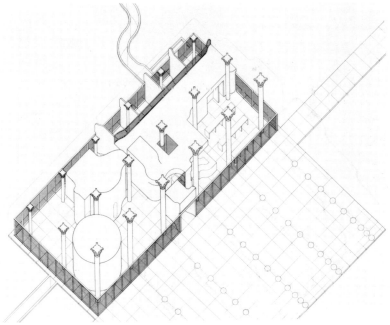

Breakaway axonometric

View toward Baha'i Temple

Interior

the Hebrews called *Kabod*) "among the ancient Hebrews took an awesome form, alien to Greek and Roman experience." Clearly the dichotomy between the Hebrew idea that man is created in the image of God and the Hellenic that God is created in the image of man has plagued the art of representation throughout history. Loerke continues: "To create an image adequate to the full force and meaning of the *Kabod-doxa* meant that the pictorial means of Greco-Roman art had to be deployed to Hebraic ends. A cultural divide had to be crossed." This cultural divide lay between the spatiality and the temporality that resulted from the two interpretations of man's encounter with God, which Loerke describes as "pro-

tective, informative and character-building" for the Greeks and "awesome" and "stunning" for the Jews.

Whenever Post-Modernism involves itself with historical precedent and uses fragmentation to depict this involvement the study of opposites follows. In the talmudic sense, study exists for its own sake with no reward beyond the study itself. There was an equivalent lack of position taking in the ruptured and agitated life of America in the 1960s and 1970s and this was inevitably reflected in architecture.

The first project in which I express these cultural concepts architecturally—The Little House in the Clouds—was made for an exhibition organized by a group of Chicago architects

D.O.M. Competition Corporate
Headquarters Project, Bruehl
(Cologne), West Germany, 1980

Assisted by Robert Fugman,
Philip Holden, Michael Abbott,
Deborah Doyle, Patrick Burke,
Ian Stewart

Photography of models:
Orlando Cabanban

A primary concern for this project
has been to achieve order through
the use of symmetry. The existing
buildings now contain new meaning and value while the focal point
of this revamped complex is the
new administration building.

The administration building is a
perfect cube of 29 meters that sits
on a plinth which is placed within
a square surrounded by a stainless
steel pergola with water running
underneath it. It is clad in a grid
of polished pink granite and pink
mirrored glass. The strong gridding makes it scaleless, and only
the windows, barely visible during
the day, give away the positions of
the floors. Along the entire length
of the axis is a golden yellow cut
4.2 meters wide that slices
through the pergola and the
building. The inside of the
anonymous mask is now revealed
through clear glass and the sensuousness of the interior workings
are unmasked. The pergola-
and-water theme is carried
through on the roof of the building, to connect heaven with earth.
The functions of the building are
split in two, quite naturally, by the
program. The south half is the
public arena. It faces the direction
in which visitors will arrive and
consists of the five sales divisions,
the reception hall and the product
presentation area. The north half
of the building, facing the factory,

Model

is the private arena of accounting,
computing, designing, directing
and training. Thus the building is
split between those who represent
the company and interact with the
outside world and those who
technically and managerially operate the company.

Two elevators link the halves.
They become the sign for the
building, traveling up and down
and highlighting the essential intricacy and movement of the
D.O.M. product. Access to the
private half of the building from
the public half is through the
elevator, which in itself becomes a
security lock. The elevators also
reinforce the building's ambiguity; from afar the building is a
cube, but as one approaches it, it
splits in two.

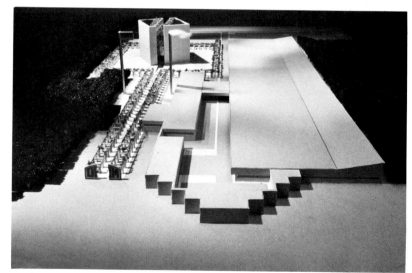

Model

Model

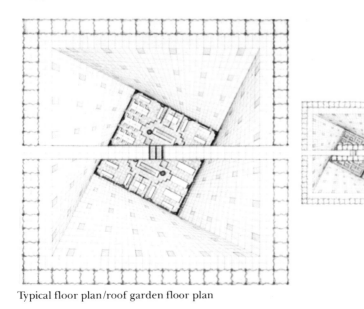

Typical floor plan/roof garden floor plan

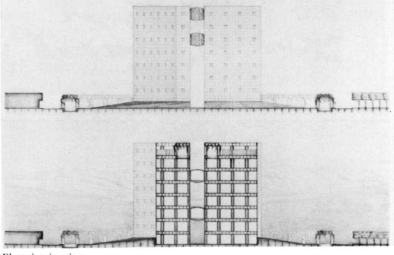

Elevation/section

Private Residence, Barrington
Hills, Illinois, 1980–81

Associate in charge:
Robert Fugman
Assisted by George Hogan,
Andrew Koglin, Deborah Doyle
Mechanical engineer:
Wallace & Migdal
Structural engineer:
Raymond Beebe
Photography of models:
Orlando Cabanban

A project concerned with dualistic
thought, its "entrance" concept is
in the embracing classical terms of
the Villas Madama and Giulia.
This concept is opposed by the
metaphor of the house as a village
(the vernacular). The "village" is
actually a series of sixteen-foot
wide gable-roof volumes whose
sacred forms are intersected by
profane functional elements.

Model

Model

Model

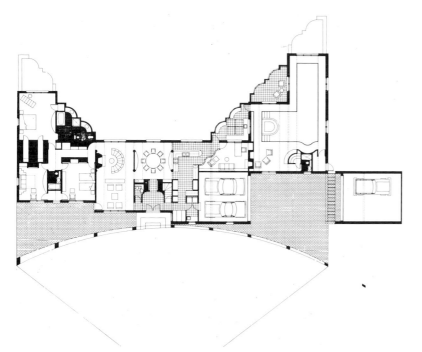

Floor plan

Model

to show their work in contradistinction to that of the Chicago Mies orthodoxy. The Little House in the Clouds interprets ideas I found in the architectural historian Joseph Rykwert's book *On Adam's House in Paradise*. The project concerns a part of American life that is independent and free and that does not have to look to Europe for meaning. My search for historical precedent was broadened in the Baha'i Archives Center of 1976–82 in Wilmette, Illinois, a repository for Baha'i archeological and historical documents. It was sited next to the Baha'i Temple, a well-known landmark, and so clearly was meant to celebrate—and be subservient to—the older building. I reinforced the nine axes of the Baha'i faith by placing the building on both sides of, but not actually on, one of these axes. People walking on that axis can thus observe an undefined future or the temple itself. The archives building would "inhabit the poché." By building on only one side of the axis and mirroring the structure with a topiary on the other, I hoped to evoke man's original and perpetual home.

Once a building is pulled apart and left apart, it is possible to extend that notion conceptually to the next stage—that of shear. The Visitor's Center for the vestigial Shaker community at Shakertown, Pleasant Hill, Kentucky, of 1979 was sheared into two pieces placed a quarter of a mile apart. Only by observing the two halves on axis with each other could they be reassembled into a recognizable solid. The purpose was to imply the poignancy of the Shaker cult whose families were split apart for communal purposes (note the doubling up of everything in their architecture—stairs, dormitory rooms, etc.).

Another project that deals with the study of opposites is the competition entry for the corporate headquarters of a company that designs precision instruments at Bruehl, outside Cologne, West Germany. Loaded with programmatic splits (capitalist managers vs. the workers), the project seemed ideal for replicating Tafuri's Deathly Mask of Silence. A Platonic solid (cube) is ruptured by a Yellow Brick Road, on one side of which is the original factory and on the other a topiary inversion. The image is of a mask—a Platonic screen—which conceals the nature of the activity behind it, but the mask is then ripped apart along an axis established by the path of the rising and setting sun. The tension formed by the desire to create a perfect state of being on the one hand and the wish to destroy that state on the other is basic to my

Entrance axonometric

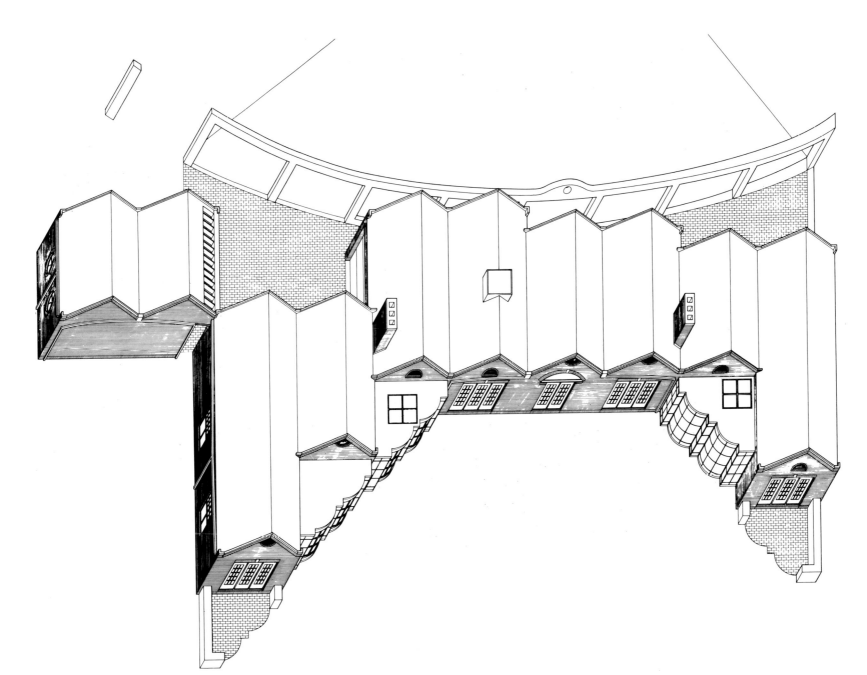

Garden axonometric

A Symbolic Museum for a Painting That Will Never Go There, Guernica, Spain, 1981

Assisted by Margaret I. McCurry, Robert Fugman, Philip Holden, Michael Abbott, Jean Norman and Andrew Koglin

The symbolic purpose of the Guernica Museum is twofold: to remind us of the bombing of Guernica, which changed the world as we knew it, and to depict the basic human optimism that somehow prevails in the face of such events. The Plaza de la Union has been ruptured along the path the German bombers took as they flew toward the sea and returned to make run after run on the people and animals assembled there. The wall of the plaza is ruptured as are five Platonic solids representing ideal and perpetual values—the cone, pyramid, cylinder, cube and sphere. The top halves of the Platonic solids rise from the glass roof of the museum. Made of polished blood-red granite, they reveal their geologic features in the ruptured areas. The wall at the underground museum level is also made of blood-red granite, symbolizing a lost ideality. The lower halves of the ruptured Platonic solids come to rest on a grass floor and are made of the same granite. It is as if the earth itself had been sheared by the hostile act wrought upon it. The lower grass level is, in fact, a park for the citizens of Guernica. This level is presented as a profane space while the upper plaza is presented as a sacred space. The rup-

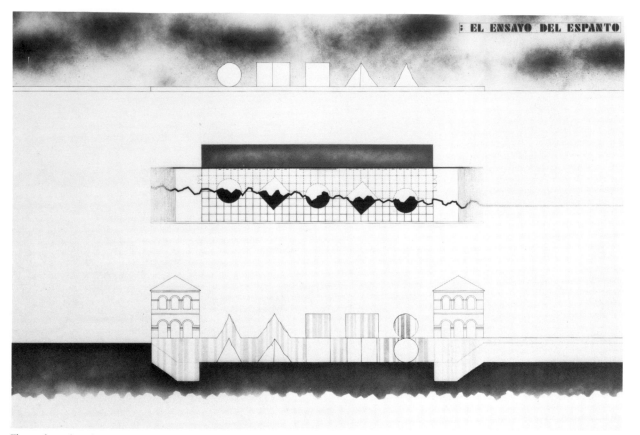

Floor plan, elevations

ture between the two represents the struggle between those disparate aspects of the human condition.

Inside the linear museum the opaque ceiling sections at the five points of the half-Platonic solids block out the sky, reminding us forever of the path of the German bombers. On the flat interior wall of the museum, "negative" reproductions of the final painting and of the sketches—black on black—are hung, as if to hide that infamous event of 1937 in the shadows of history.

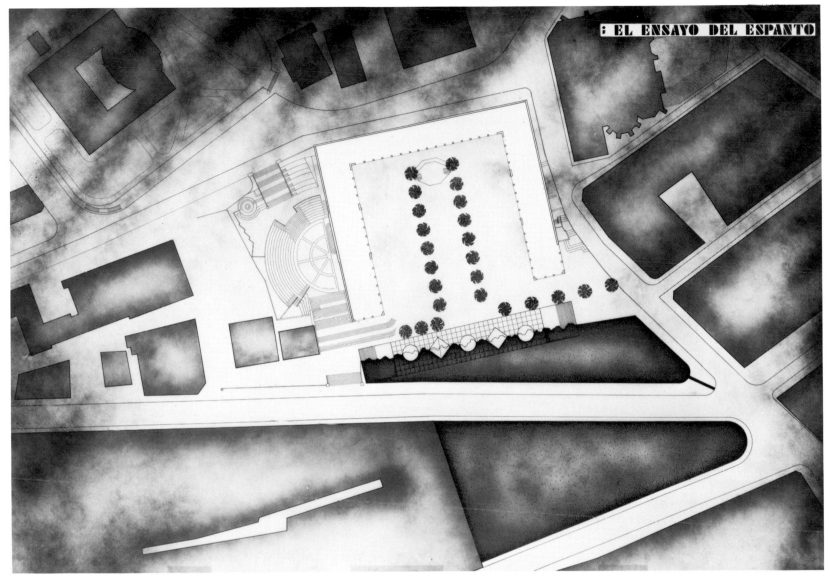

¡ EL ENSAYO DEL ESPANTO

Site plan

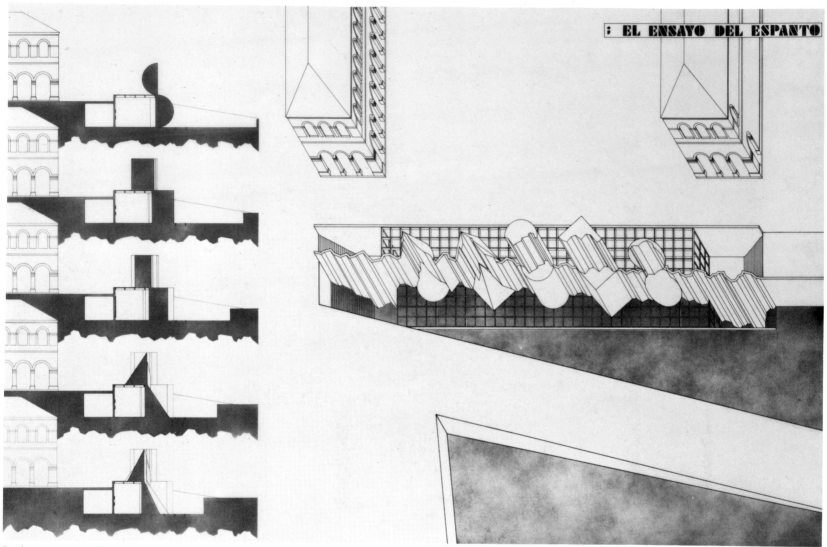

Sections, axonometrics

work in this section. It is analogous to the tension that exists between biblical morality and the flawed world of built form (Eliade's "cosmicization").

The private residence in Barrington Hills, Illinois, of 1980–81 is more subtle in its use of inverted elements because elements of a different order are used. Here classical and vernacular elements are juxtaposed, showing that they can exist together in the same epoch.

In designing a museum for Guernica, Spain, I followed Picasso's lead when he emotionally responded to the German bombing of that Basque town by painting *Guernica* in 1937

and rupturing the Platonic ideal. In my building I rupture five Platonic solids along the actual path the German bombers took. These broken solids are juxtaposed with a Cartesian glass grid skylight, which is above the underground museum designed to house a painting that will never go there (Picasso stipulated that *Guernica* hang in perpetuity at the Prado in Madrid). Man's inhumanity to man is thus symbolized by describing the boundary between the sacred and the profane.

As in The Little House in the Clouds, forms are deployed along both sides of a Yellow Brick Road without resolution or

Exhibition, Thonet Showroom,
The Merchandise Mart, Chicago,
Illinois, 1981

Assisted by Robert Fugman,
Andrew Koglin, Peter
Hawrylewicz, Angela Morgan

Photography: Sadin Karant

Constructions:
Countryside Cabinets

A built example illustrating concerns with inversion, reversal, dualism, incompleteness—with the dialectic of Post-Modernism as a Jewish Movement.

Showroom entrance

synthesis in the 1981 Thonet exhibition. Participation is involved here for resolution. Although I deal up to a point with resolution in this project, I don't believe it has to be explicit in order to convey formal and symbolic messages. In any case responses to the same hypothesis inevitably differ according to time and circumstances and so resolution is in a constant state of flux.

Throughout history objectivity and subjectivity have waged battle over which would represent a given culture at a given time. We have just come through a period in which the victor was idealist objectivity. During this era Modernist preoccupations with the ideal therefore ruled out involvement with the particular and idiosyncratic in life. Depersonalization was the manner of the times.

This detachment extended to critics and historians of the period as well. The art historian James S. Ackerman has pointed out in an unpublished paper, *Interpretation, Response: Suggestions for a Theory of Art Criticism:* "Cubism, International Style architecture and their descendants in the 1950s were the modern restatements of the classical tradition. Critical theory perfectly complemented the asceticism and purism of

early twentieth century art in enjoining the critic and historian from engaging with the art object." This is reminiscent of Kierkegaard's detached view of "aesthetic man." In Kierkegaard's statement that "to exist as a human being means to exist ethically and to face perpetually new moral choices" can be seen the crux of the problem of Modernist architectural dogma: the precluding of the taking of more than one point of view at a time.

In his book *Dostoevsky, Kierkegaard, Nietzsche and Kafka,* William Hubben underscores Kierkegaard's ethically religious position in this dialectic: "The essential condition of the never-ending process of becoming a Christian is, according to Kierkegaard, unrest, unpeace of mind, and insecurity—an internal motion to be borne only in prayer and repentance, during which the individual stands 'before God' in solitude."

Kierkegaard's separation of the "aesthetic man," who is detached from life and lives out a dream world, from the moral man, who endlessly struggles in the "process of becoming," evolved from his own internal battle as a younger man when he wrote in his diaries: "I too have both the tragic and

View of showroom

Author's memorial service

the comic in me: I am witty and the people laugh—but I cry."

The concept of opposites in which one side enriches the other (by implication) has its origins in Aristotelian logic. The dual methods of explaining life (Platonic abstraction vs. Aristotelian concretization) have been at the source of architectural conflict throughout history. Yet Aristotle contended that both methods ought to be considered and that if there must be synthesis it should occur in the mean between the opposites—not in the fact of one being victorious over the other. In proposing an ideal life based on the Aristotelian Doctrine of the Mean, Maimonides talked of a balanced, symmetrical life in which the Hellenic trust in beauty would be applied to the Hebraic faith in moral duty.

Platonic theory holds forth the concept of perfection—the notion that architects refer to as "the spirit of all the ages." All human beings have a wish, in part, to leave their "footprints" for posterity to see. But in the very concept of the perpetual lies the suggestion that life on earth is less than ideal. Most historically legitimate architectural monuments were built with the ideal in mind, but they were also built simply as representations of their own times. Dualistic attitudes represented by both the finite and the infinite bring to mind a Kierkegaardian notion: "He who lives ethically has memory of his life, whereas he who lives aesthetically has not." Only those who seek moral ideals thus "exist." Morality enters any discussion concerning Platonic ideals when totemistic, holistic, iconic concerns about perpetuity are presented as outweighing the simple representation of life itself, however flawed. America vintage 1960–80 was more Hebraic than Hellenic in dealing with the problems of irony, frailty and schizophrenia—in a word, the problems of life and death, of humanity.

Modern life continues to demand multiple roles, and the contemporary conflict between idealism and realism is every bit as much a tug-of-war as the traditional battle between the classical and the vernacular. In Judaism one is taught that by being a martyr one is a saint; ethics are not taught in terms of ideality and the goal is not the end point. (It's not a matter of whether you win or lose, it's how you play the game.) Talmudic reasoning does not suggest synthesis; it is based instead on the fact of being torn this way and that and the implications each side has for the other. The "Torah is at once hidden and manifest, esoteric and exoteric." By concentrating on this world and not the next, it is possible in architecture to achieve an imperfect form of building representing the imperfect anthropomorphic condition of man—and this is central to my argument. In Judaism the basic question of morality is one of constant debate with oneself. In his book on *The Living Talmud* Judah Goldin writes of the tensions the Talmud preserves: "Views in conflict, argument advancing and withdrawing, contradictions harmonized only with acutest dialectic, diverse subjects made to reveal underlying unifying principles, the movement of the mind from theme to theme, and the succession of generations of scholars seeking for the new developments and insights sanctioned by the old." Even Nietzsche reinforced these tensions by saying: "I believe only by doubting whether I believe."

It is perfectly possible in one building to have a dialectic between the Platonic striving for perfection and the perverse desire to rupture that very perfection in order to represent the frailty of the human condition. This dualism reflects the disparate forces man continuously faces. Concerns about inversion and reversal can be found in Ecclesiastes: "There is a time for everything: a time to be born and a time to die; a time to plant and a time to uproot; a time to kill and a time to heal; a time to break down and a time to build up; a time to weep and a time to laugh; a time to mourn and a time to dance; a time to cast away stones and a time to gather stones; a time to embrace and a time to repel; a time to seek and a time to discard; a time to keep and a time to throw away; a time to rend and a time to mend; a time to keep silent and a time to speak; a time to love and a time to hate; a time for war and a time for peace" (Philip Birnbaum, *The Concise Jewish Bible*).

The Talmud's attempts at interpreting the Torah confirm the Ecclesiastian dialectic. In his book *The Essential Talmud* Adin Steinsaltz explains: "No individual can study [the] Talmud without being or becoming an eternal skeptic." In describing the individual's constant search for truth, Steinsaltz goes on to comment: "This attitude also explains the untiring search for the alternate dimension of things. The refusal to remain content with simplistic solutions generates the desire to see matters in a different light. The critical sense is later levelled at social, scientific and economic problems and sometimes creates the spark of genius that can reveal the 'other possibility,' the opposite of the existing order."

Fashion and change are not the repugnant phenomena architects accuse them of being. They merely stand in the way of the Zeitgeist mentality that wishes to preserve the status quo no matter what the facts of the matter are. Fashion and change are used by civilization to express motion within the modalities of the times. In contradistinction, the ideal is used by mankind to express perpetuity (Eliade's paradigmatic godliness). The struggle between these polarities is what life is all about. I believe that architecture is about this very same struggle. Ecclesiastes: "I know that there is nothing better for men than to be happy and enjoy themselves as long as they are alive. It is indeed God's very gift to man that he should eat and drink and be happy as he toils. There is one fate for man and beast; as the one dies so the other dies; the same breath is in all of them. All go to one place; all are from dust and all return to the dust. Who knows whether the spirit of man goes upward and the spirit of the beast goes down to the earth? So I saw that it is best for man to enjoy his work and be happy" (Philip Birnbaum, *The Concise Jewish Bible*).

Death as end point suggests that irony is nothing more than a fact of life. In architecture, irony, not by itself evil, may be employed to express simultaneity as opposed to synthesis. Although it can be argued that synthesis is an attempt at godliness, in the Bible Isaiah states something quite different: "My thoughts are not like your thoughts, nor are your ways like my ways, says the Lord. As the heavens are higher than the earth, so are my ways higher than your ways and my thoughts than your thoughts. As the rain and the snow come down from heaven and return not thither, but water the earth and make it yield seed for the sower and bread for the eater, so is the word that comes forth from my mouth; it does not return to me fruitless but carries out the plan for which I sent it" (ibid).

An architecture that employs images exclusively to communicate symbolic content is in contradiction with that part of Exodus wherein God states: "You shall have no other Gods beside me. You shall not make for yourself any idols in the shape of anything that is in heaven above, or that is on the earth below, or that is in the water under the earth. You shall not bow down to them nor worship them; for I, the Lord your God, am a jealous God, punishing children for the sins of their fathers, down to the third or fourth generation of those who hate me, but showing kindness in the thousandth generation of those who love me and keep my commandments" (ibid).

The forbidding of extrinsic image-making in Exodus reflects the famous myth wherein Abraham destroys the idols his father had made. The psychoanalyst Silvano Arieti points out in his book *Abraham and the Contemporary Mind* that "with the breaking of the idols, a new era starts. Abraham is the first Jew, and he is the founder of the modern world, a world that will painfully, throughout centuries and centuries, try to overcome primitive feeling, thinking, acting and all the various forms of idolatry that are connected with them."

An architecture that is employed strictly in the service of perpetual values cannot contend with the sanctification of life. Just as Kierkegaard celebrated ethical man "in the process of becoming," one may celebrate man's work in the same "process of becoming." Arieti reinforces this point: "In Jewish doctrine, life on earth counts, too, and what I as an individual do has an eternal effect not only on my soul but on earth as well. Thus the human being must strive to sanctify life" (*Abraham and the Contemporary Mind*). If, as Mies van der Rohe said, "architecture is the will of an epoch translated into space," then architecture should be among the disciplines that interprets the dualistic tendencies expressed by contemporary civilization. Arieti states: "Dualism finds its first expression in Abraham's separation of God from nature. What is implied by this dualism is an ultimate principle that transcends the physical, even if the manifestations of this principle are required to interact with the physical. Even if the mental is required to arise from the physical, it goes beyond the physical and bespeaks something that comes before and after the physical. Only man is able to receive by intuition or revelation the existence of this ultimate principle; and because of this ability he can be conceived as being made in the image of God. To accept Abraham's dualism and interactionism means also to accept the interaction between God and the world, God and the human being" (*Abraham and the Contemporary Mind*). Dualism is open to change and is without bias, and it posits the possible. It is about life and death and hope. It is interpretive and suggestive and therefore is of architecture.

Lest the reader mistakenly construe that the attitudes found in Chapter 9 represent The Answer, he or she should recall that in each of the earlier chapters, the attitudes too were thought to be The Answer at the time they occurred. The distance I appear to have achieved from the work of the earlier chapters is based on the passage of time and the evolution of society. The ideas embodied in Chapter 9 exist by virtue of my current perception of culture, and since each prior chapter begat the next, it strikes me as implicit that as time continues to pass and society continues to change, Chapter 9 will beget Chapter 10, Chapter 10 will beget Chapter 11, ad infinitum.

On the other hand...

Stanley Tigerman: The Education of a Chicago Architect

by Ross Miller

Stanley Tigerman's architecture is rooted in the city of Chicago. Like the city itself, his work has a legitimate and illegitimate history. On the legitimate side it owes a subtle kind of debt to John Root, Louis Sullivan and Frank Lloyd Wright as well as to more eclectic and lesser known Chicago architects: Andrew Rebori, David Adler and George Fred Keck. However, on the other side Tigerman can be seen as an indirect descendant of, an heir to, another kind of Chicago history—from George Ade through Al Capone and Abbie Hoffman—whereby he is attentive to a growing source of myth and drama. For there is quite a strange collision of forces and influences at the center of Stanley Tigerman's career. Tigerman's precarious balancing act between the legitimate and the illegitimate—the purely abstract and the simply empirical, the classical and the vernacular—makes him unusually sensitive to the ever-changing character of American architecture. His own work, while mindful of formal restraints, implies that building is more than the massing of forms and the creation of volumes; it tends toward the formulation of a colloquial American architectural style where formal usage is twisted and reshaped to communicate beyond pure spaces and geometries. This style develops from the idiosyncrasies of the architect, the urban environment and the accidents of Chicago history.

The history of Chicago seems to encourage the linking of improbable contradictions: appearing simultaneously self-aggrandized and deflated. This section of land along Lake

Michigan, named Fort Dearborn in 1803, was called by the Indians *Chicagou* or *Chicagow*, meaning bad stink. By 1812 the Indians, acting as agents of the British, thought enough of Chicago to burn down the fort. However, owing to its excellent location the fort was rebuilt and the place flourished. The port of Chicago opened in 1830 and the town was incorporated in 1833. Due to the rapid growth of population, Fort Dearborn was abandoned as a frontier outpost within four years, and the town was made a city incorporating one hundred square miles. Throughout the mid-nineteenth century Chicago continued to draw people from the East— newly arrived immigrants—and became a transit point for Western traders. Builders, attempting to accommodate the rush of population, began Chicago's glorious architectural history on a less than glorious note. Adept at prefabricated construction, in improvising on the flexible balloon frame,[1] developers provided business space and housing. By the late 1830s wood plank streets were raised, jacked up as much as twelve feet above the swampy land, and haphazardly constructed buildings were added. By 1855 twelve thousand acres had been developed in this manner; ten railroads terminated in this city of eighty thousand called informally Slabtown or Mudtown.

Within eight years another twenty-four square miles were added and the population had doubled. Chicago became the main stop to the West by land or inland waterways, and a banking (mostly New York and Boston institutions) and real estate center for Western land speculation. The Civil War provided an almost unlimited market for the city's grain and livestock traders. Entrepreneurs like McCormick, Palmer, Field, Armour and Swift found Chicago—Urbs in Horto as commercial promoters called her—an open place to work. Before the Great Fire, Otto von Bismarck was quoted as saying "I wish I could go to America if only to see Chicago."[2] The place would naturally inspire Bismarckian awe because of its extraordinary vitality and rapid development. It grew out of nothing, in the middle of nowhere, from an army post to a world city in less than seventy years. And yet it was the Chicago Fire (1871) that forever united the entrepreneur— the city builder and Bismarckian ideal—with the architect.[3]

If Chicago had a mythic history, Samarkand on the swamp, before the fire, its phoenixlike rebirth—an almost complete rebuilding—made it seem even more special during the last two decades of the century. The new city (post-1871) was so different from the old that it appeared created anew, not to have evolved, as most cities do, but made over.[4] This rapid transformation had a direct effect on the architecture that continues to motivate the Chicago architects of today— particularly one as sensitive to shifting trends as Stanley Tigerman. It presented the opportunity for dramatic change, a chance for an architect to build what he imagined. Chicago as a place to experiment and design—dynamic enough to accommodate speculation and conflict—has supported through its history a strange mix of personalities.

To Root, Sullivan and Wright, Stanley Tigerman owes almost no architectural debt, but as a product of Chicago (born and raised in the city) he learned something much more refractory from them. Tigerman, while avoiding their style, has the paradoxical mixture of the idealist and the practical spirit of the entrepreneurial builder that motivated the first great group of Chicago architects, architects who made the extraarchitectural intent of their work as important as the built piece. Building to them was not only a fact of industrial life but a thing *willed* into being. It had meaning, as Tigerman insists too, beyond the work's specific program.

Louis Sullivan, for instance, as his career developed, increasingly began to see architecture as an occult form of autobiography where the individual artist's will could be known through the mute materials of architecture. Building to him was an inchoate form of language marrying unlikely opposites: the intensely private with the coldly public, willed yet determined. "I have a dawning suspicion that making a real building, as you would call it, and making a real poem, are pretty much one and the same thing."[5] Later, referring directly to the development of the tall office building about which he was ambivalent, Sullivan said, "The architectural art...would certainly become a living form of speech."[6] Sullivan, however, was not the only architect of his generation to see the special "literary" opportunities presented by Chicago after the Fire. John Root, though more conservative than Louis Sullivan, as partner of Daniel Burnham realized that being an architect in Chicago allowed one to express himself beyond the straight job of building. Although Root, unlike Sullivan who was quick to seize the autobiographical aspect of architecture, knew there was something special about his role, he was not sure what to call it:

Here the pure art expression can, perhaps, never be so high as in the simpler problem, for reasons inherent in the problem; but if it is to be truly an art expression worth considering, it will be reached at the point where intellectual action, intensely concentrated upon vital conditions about and within us, passes into an unconscious spiritual clairvoyance.[7]

There was something different about the place even if he could not quite get it down in words. The heady experience of rebuilding a city[8] using the best of modern technology—steel frame, reinforced foundations, new fenestration, electric appliances, elevators and lights—was coupled with the possibility that the individual architect could be known through these forms. For Frank Lloyd Wright architecture might once again become the principal form of communication, only this time more personal, never again to be anonymous: "Thus down to the time of Gutenberg architecture is the principal writing—the universal writing of humanity."[9] Here again, although Wright is a little more circumspect and therefore more of a survivor than Sullivan, he stops short of calling modern architecture autobiographical. But he uses similar imagery and refers to it as a form of "writing." What John Root called communal expression—"The large office building in Chicago…the subject is chosen because no class of buildings is more expressive of modern life in its complexity, its luxury, its intense vitality[10]—Louis Sullivan called a very personal form of discourse where the architect's tone and voice express the will of the many:

> In other words, if we would know why certain things are as they are in our disheartening architecture, we must look to the people; for our buildings, as a whole, are but a huge screen behind which are our people as a whole—even though specifically the buildings are individual images of those to whom, as a class, the public has delegated and entrusted its power to build.[11]

Sullivan stands immediately behind the building, a screen upon which he projects his own idiosyncrasies and ideas; the building and he are identified as one.

The Chicago architect of the 1890s sponsored a very ambitious conceit. Paul Bourget, a French visitor to the city in 1893, fascinated with the energy of the place, observed the architecture and found it particularly unsettling. He wrote in *Outre-Mer:*

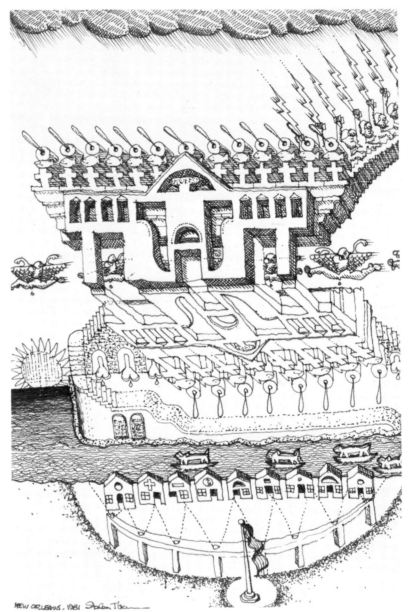

New Orleans, Louisiana, 1981

167

Men! The word is hardly correct applied to this perplexing city. When you study it more in detail, its aspect reveals so little of the personal will, so little caprice and individuality, in its streets and buildings, that it seems like the work of some impersonal power, irresistible, unconscious like a force of nature, in whose service man was merely a passive instrument.[12]

Bourget and other contemporaries were quick to recognize the paradoxical nature of Chicago architecture, seemingly so puritanically wedded to the community and so fiercely the object of the speculator in commercial real estate. It is not unusual that the architect and the journalist would not see it exactly the same way. But this self-serving fiction of the architect seeing himself expressed directly, "written" into the building, gradually disappeared over the first twenty years of this century as architecture developed more to meet the market place than to serve the ideals of "democratic building."[13]

However, the force and influence of Root, Sullivan and Wright's rhetoric should not be underestimated. It affects the way contemporary architects view and present their work. In fact, now that the more personal, individuated side of architecture is almost entirely divorced from the practical day-to-day requirements of building, the more conceptual or abstract side of Chicago architecture flourishes. Stanley Tigerman, admittedly on a smaller scale—mostly in domestic rather than public commissions—has revived, albeit in a different form, an essential yet dormant tradition in Chicago architecture. He has put ideas—what Root called "intellectual action," Sullivan called "autobiographical" and Wright called "writing"—back into a contemporary architectural practice.

Stanley Tigerman's intellectual development draws in a subliminal way on the first generation of Chicago architects, although the actual form and content of his practice are influenced more directly by circumstances of education, types of commissions and the vagaries of popular culture. Again, like Chicago itself, his attention is divided between the lure of high style and ideas—the legacy of Root, Sullivan and Wright—and the existential demands of a living city. St. Benedict's Abbey Church, Instant City and Kelmer Arlington Industrial Building—all a little too serious and self-conscious—are part of the same body of work as Hot Dog House, Animal Crackers and Tigerman Takes a Bite Out of Keck. Only in truly conceptual works like The Little House in the Clouds, The Best Home of All and The Great American Cemetery, or in projects like his notorious pornographic Daisy House, Baha'i Archives Center, Sam's Cut-Rate Liquors, Anti-Cruelty Society and the Illinois Regional Library, where the specific local requirements of a commisison are met by an equally inventive solution, does Tigerman build at the level he thinks. The results are colloquial, informal and almost conversational in the way the architecture communicates. Tigerman's best work is what Sullivan called an "utterance" that solves the particular problems of a commission while "speaking" to the larger questions of architecture. But Tigerman is unfortunately reticent in his use of the colloquial style.[14] He is still in the process of integrating "serious" modern design (learned at Yale and preached at the Institute for Architecture and Urban Studies) with more informal ideas that have more to do with autobiography, dreams and literature than they do academic architecture.

Tigerman, like other Chicagoans before him, is intensely uncomfortable with the doubleness of Chicago life—to be an artist and accessible, idealistic yet commercial, amusing but taken seriously. Other cities do not create this problem. In New York an artist is serious. Tigerman's years in school taught him that. Paul Rudolph, Louis Kahn, John Hejduk are *serious* God knows. Even Robert Venturi is serious. So is Las Vegas once he gets to it. Tigerman learned to build important structures. The Metal and Glass House and Urban Matrix are New York-inspired works. He tends to call them "boring" now because there is another strong influence on his career. He is affected by another city: Los Angeles. There an architect is not supposed to be serious, and is thought best when, like Frank Gehry, Craig Hodgetts and Frank Israel, he engages the conceptual—dare one say whimsical—play of his mind.

Tigerman is most unconventional and original—really at *his* best—when he combines both influences. He again becomes a Chicago architect who views his position ironically—between two coasts, two opposite, charged poles of contemporary architectural influence—and builds.[15]

Tigerman, at first, appears unusually conflicted in his approach to his work. In fact, there does not appear to be any

Montreal, Quebec, 1981

simple unity or immediately recognizable direction to his architecture. As I have noted there are strong historical and contemporary reasons for this eclecticism. I would like now to speculate as to the reasons for this development as it pertains to the immediate postwar architectural environment in Chicago and to suggest a more general explanation implicit in the special development of the city. The former concerns Stanley Tigerman's reaction to the work of Mies van der Rohe and the latter involves the larger Chicago culture of which Tigerman as an architect and popular critic is part.

As early as the turn-of-the-century, novelists like Theodore Dreiser and Frank Norris described the strange awkwardness of Chicago life. Frank Norris writes in *The Pit* of a night at the opera. He pictures women in expensive gowns, men in evening clothes, trying to engage the seriousness of the moment. But try as they will they are unable to overcome the crowd's coarseness. Art is only a minor distraction for the businessman:

Why could not men leave their business outside, why must the jar of commerce spoil all the harmony of this moment. However, all sounds were drowned suddenly in a long burst of applause. The tenor and soprano bowed and smiled across the footlights. The soprano vanished, only to reappear on the balcony of the pavilion, and while she declared that the stars and the nightbird together sang "He loves thee," the voices close at hand continued:
"—— one hundred and six carloads——"
"—— paralyzed the bulls——"
"—— fifty thousand dollars——"
Then all at once the lights went up. The act was over.[16]

Norman Mailer notes the same kind of tension between the desire for respectability and the essential "carnal" energy of the city. In *Miami and the Siege of Chicago* he calls Chicago "the great American city," and argues that the product of this conflict is creative:

Chicago did not have Manhattan to preempt top

Napa, California, 1981

branches, so it grew up from the savory of its neighborhoods to some of the best high-rise architecture in the world, and because its people were Poles and Ukrainians and Czechs as well as Irish and the rest, the city had Byzantine corners worthy of Prague or Moscow, odd tortured attractive drawbridges over the Chicago River, huge Gothic spires like the skyscraper which held the Chicago *Tribune,* curves and abutments and balconies in cylindrical structures thirty stories high twisting in and out of the curves of the river, and fine balustrades in its parks.... In superb back streets behind the towers on the lake were brownstones which spoke of ironies, cupidities and intricate ambition in the fists of the robber barons who commissioned them—substantiality, hard work, heavy drinking, carnal meats of pleasure, and a Midwestern sense of how to arrive at upper-class decorum were also in the American grandeur of the few streets.[17]

But I believe it is Saul Bellow, like Tigerman a lifelong resident of Chicago, who sees clearest the conflict between the native, ironic, colloquial energies of the city and the almost comical need for respectability in purely architectural terms. He describes, in *Dangling Man,* a man-made Chicago environment that Tigerman, as his career develops, increasingly addresses. Today, the heroic balance between individual intent as manifested in personal ways by Root, Sullivan and Wright and the demands of the marketplace can no longer be assumed. The scales are tipped. To this point Bellow has his central character react to a letter from a friend, John Pearl, who has just left Chicago for New York:

"Peeling furniture, peeling walls, posters, bridges, everything is peeling and scaling in South Brooklyn. We moved here to save money, but I'm afraid we'd better start saving ourselves and move out again. It's the treelessness, as much as anything, that hurts me. *The unnatural, too-human deadness.*"

I'm sorry for him. I know what he feels, the kind of terror, and the danger he sees of *the lack of the human in the too-human.* We find it, as others before us have found it in the last two hundred years, and we bolt for "Nature." It happens in all cities. And *cities are "natural," too.* He thinks he would be safer in Chicago, where he grew up. Sentimentality! He doesn't mean Chicago. It is no less inhuman.[18] (Emphasis mine)

It is Stanley Tigerman's response to Chicago's "lack of the human in the too-human," and particularly his reaction to the work of Mies van der Rohe, that completes his education as a Chicago architect and drives him to develop his own colloquial style.

When Mies arrived in Chicago (1938) to head the Armour Institute, later renamed the Illinois Institute of Technology, he brought with him many years of experience in European Modernism and a tested architectural methodology. His influence upon the city was immediate and profound. Aided later by the postwar building boom, under the guidance of czarlike Mayor Richard Daley, Chicago became completely identified with the universal curtain-walled, steel-framed, loft spaces of Mies.[19] Ironically, Chicago, which prided itself on the ingenuity and variety of its architecture, was now expressed by a single style, damned by the sheer mindless repetition of grand flat-topped high-rises.

Stanley Tigerman, perhaps as a partial answer to those who would propose one kind of architecture for a city as diverse as Chicago, helped put together a show, in 1976, that exhibited a varied body of work, primarily by architects who practiced in the years after the ascendancy of the First Chicago School (1871–1900) and before the arrival of Mies. He and fellow architects Laurence Booth, Stuart Cohen and Benjamin Weese re-introduced Andrew Rebori, David Adler and George Fred Keck, among others, who had been more or less lost in the move toward Miesian architecture. The work is surprisingly varied and filled with indigenous solutions to special Chicago building problems. Rebori's architecture has a soft-edged Moderne look to it; Adler is a home-grown historicist designer; and George Fred Keck is an early prairie Modernist. There are a lot of good designs, some merely quirky or bizarre. But the importance of the show is clearer now in retrospect. I think it was more Tigerman's own unilateral declaration of stalemate than a full response to the direct challenge by Miesian Chicago architecture. The show and book[20] correctly criticized the "idea-less" state of

Miesian architecture—"Build. Don't talk."—but did not replace it with any compelling idea of its own. For as interesting and potentially significant as some of the work—new and old—was in *Chicago Architects,* none of it really addressed the central question. It rightly criticized Mies for favoring one side of the city's schizophrenic personality without articulating the other. Mies and his followers—almost 100% of the postwar building up to the master's death (1969) used a Miesian system—made Chicago look too "legit." Stanley Tigerman, of course, understands this. Unfortunately, however, the grab bag of "eclectics" Tigerman was championing, although more sensitive to the indigenous possibilities of architecture and certainly more diverse, was still not capable of the kind of synthesis between the legitimate look of a formal style and the particular flavor or drama of Chicago. If Mies was Chicago's Goliath there was no single architect—settled enough in his own work—to play David. The non-Miesian architectural community had scattered and appeared unarmed.

In fact, Tigerman's support of an eclectic group of architects simply reflects his own drift into eclecticism—as if resisting one system led him to resist all[21]—during the late 1960s and mid-1970s. So at once he is designing a high-technology Metal and Glass House and then a glum brick box with rounded corners, an "incubator building" for new businesses in an industrial park. During this same period he designs Boardwalk, a perfect copy of Mies's Lafayette Park in Detroit, like William Wilson in Poe's story who becomes his double out of sheer preoccupation and anxiety.

During this decade of Tigerman's work one can observe the influence of De Stijl, Kahn, Mondrian, Mies and Disney. It would be a critical mistake to minimize this period or the ideas that motivated it. In a way Tigerman's race through a catalogue of styles was his most profound response to Mies or any proponent of a single architectural method.[22] Although there are problems with some of these designs individually, when taken together over time they appear no less arbitrary than architecture that sticks blindly to a rigid, preordained and self-imposed orthodoxy.

Tigerman's experimentation has led him to rethink the way contemporary architects should operate. Some of these experiments have already found their way into his built work and some are now purely conceptual. In his attempt to have architecture again deal with ideas, Stanley Tigerman, on a much smaller scale than the turn-of-the-century Chicago architects, is attempting "to speak through his architecture." A look at some selected recent projects, built and unbuilt, will clarify the direction of his work.

It is as if Tigerman needs, for the moment, to turn his back on Mies and develop some coherent critique of the culture for which he is designing before he can add to the pure but refractory materials of architecture a clearly articulated voice like that of Sullivan or Wright.

A project for Best Products indicates his current thinking on the problem. In December, 1979, the Museum of Modern Art exhibited designs on a single problem by prominent architects practicing in America. All, among them Tigerman, Robert Stern, Michael Graves and Alan Greenberg, were asked to plan a new catalogue showroom for Best Products. Best, in the past, had commissioned SITE and Robert Venturi. Significantly, all the invited architects produced actual buildable plans or models except for Stanley Tigerman. A closer look at his scheme gives some indication why.

I think Tigerman is at a point where his ideas can no longer be contained through a series of jumps from one style to another. He is now admitting, in quite a clear way, that a contemporary architecture that returns to a mindless quoting of the past: Doric columns in narrow urban hallways and giant keystones over Mommy and Daddy's bed is one great dead end. By drawing only a picture, a conceptual rendering of a problem, he is suggesting that no complete design solution is available. In presenting The Best Home of All and asking us to contemplate the images, he provokes us to question why there is yet no contemporary architecture equal to the strange, sometimes vulgar, variety of American life.[23] Mies is simply insufficient, Post-Modernism is a name for a collection of attic oddities that are now called, by convention, "state of the art." Tigerman's work for the Best Products Show indicates a kind of silence, a momentary retreat from building to contemplate his next step.

The over-scaled images point to the absurdity of simply incorporating a serious architectural program in the suburbs and questions the whole conceit of environmental control. Frank Lloyd Wright's Prairie Houses or Usonian communities are not appropriate to a culture that is not directed from above—by Wrightian or Sullivanian pronouncements on democratic life—but seems to spawn and clone itself. In Tigerman's vision, giant mailboxes and gargantuan backboards and hoops form the American landscape. Watts Tower-size antennas wait in silence to be contacted. Tigerman understands that for Root, Sullivan and Wright—and for even a more contemporary generation of architects like Kahn, Rudolph and Hejduk—the American landscape was still more abstract, just waiting to be filled with architectural ideas. But in the absence of any generative architecture, aided by the mute and dumb Miesian idiom of speculative building, the land, with or without architects, was "developed." Robert Venturi points to this development in *Complexity and Contradiction in Architecture* in a far too sanguine way because he believes that the "vernacular" architecture of developers that crowds commercial strips and suburban lots will still admit the hand of the trained architect and designer who will make it all properly scaled, neat and legitimate. But Stanley Tigerman realizes, to his credit, that the "illegitimate"—the gross meaty side of Chicago life, for instance[24]—has a life of its own and operates by its own rules. His exhibit for Best Products reveals his understanding that even when the architectural establishment and talmudic thinkers were not watching the vernacular had taken over.[25]

American architects in the absence of any compelling idea since Louis Kahn's experiments with materials, classical masses and volumes, and without any easily communicated methodology since Mies, are left to write long scholastic digressions in magazines like *Oppositions* and *A + U* or hold art shows to sell renderings of unbuilt projects. Tigerman recognizes this retreat from the traditional role of American architecture—part pragmatic, part idealistic, evangelical and confessional—but his built work, like Wright and Sullivan's during their most polemical periods, has not yet caught up to his conceptual or literary insights.

In a recent project for the Architectural League of New York, Tigerman has collaborated with the artist Richard Haas to produce a design entitled The Great American Cemetery, which is, in effect, the urban counterpart of The Best Home of All. Three caskets are in the foreground, suburban houses are in the middleground and the urban skyline rises as a backdrop. The burial field gives way to the living death of the suburbs until it finally yields to the decay of the modern city. Again, Tigerman has made his wasteland filled with familiar images that are cut off from any possibility of communication.

These two conceptual projects, along with the earlier Little House in the Clouds, are attempts to draw back from the day-to-day practice of architecture and try to see as an outsider might the state of the profession. The fact that Tigerman recognizes the wasteland and is not yet prepared to make his move in the form of a completely realized architecture is underscored by his work at the 1980 Biennale in Venice. In a huge bay in the old rope works of the Arsenale he created a facade. By the nature of the project the facade leads nowhere and signifies nothing inside. He is experimenting with the raw process of architecture. Consistent with the hard satirical quality of much of his recent work he constructs a series of drapes, in forced perspective, leading one implacably to the emptiness inside. He encourages the visitor to enter, telling him at the same time that there is nothing to enter for.

1. Sigfried Giedion, *Space, Time and Architecture* (Cambridge, Mass., 1974), pp. 346-54.

2. Quoted by Stephen Longstreet in *Chicago, 1860–1919* (New York, 1979).

3. Daniel Burnham is the best example of this Bismarckian type. See Thomas S. Hines, *Burnham of Chicago* (New York, 1974); Charles Moore, *Daniel H. Burnham: Architect Planner of Cities* (New York, 1921); Edward Wolner, "Daniel Burnham and the Tradition of the City Builder in Chicago" (unpublished dissertation, New York University).

4. Elias Colbert and Everett Chamberlin, *Chicago and the Great Conflagration* (New York, 1871).

5. Louis H. Sullivan, *Kindergarten Chats and Other Writings* (New York, 1968), p. 87.

6. Ibid., p. 214.

7. John Wellborn Root, "A Great Architectural Problem," in *The Meanings of Architecture,* ed. Donald Hoffman (New York, 1967), p. 133.

8. For more information on the size and scope of construction in Chicago at the end of the nineteenth century see Carl W. Condit, *American Building* (Chicago, 1968); Harold M. Mayer and Richard C. Wade, *Chicago: Growth of a Metropolis* (Chicago, 1969); and *The Architectural Review,* No. 968, October, 1977.

9. Frank Lloyd Wright, "The Art and Craft of the Machine," in *Frank Lloyd Wright: Writings and Buildings,* eds. Edgar Kaufmann and Ben Raeburn (New York, 1960), p. 57.

10. Root, p. 141.

11. Sullivan, p. 24.

12. Paul Bourget, *Outre-Mer* (New York, 1895), p. 117.

13. Along with Bourget's *Outre-Mer* there are several important contemporaneous accounts of Chicago architecture. Among them are Henry Fuller, *The Cliff Dwellers* (New York, 1893); Montgomery Schuyler, *American Architecture and Other Writings* (Cambridge, 1961); G. W. Steevens, *The Land of the Dollar* (New York, 1897).

14. We can see Sullivan's experimentation with ornamentation as an extraarchitectural form of communication, a kind of "language," in his *A System of Architectural Ornamentation* (Chicago, 1924).

15. Tigerman's most successful buildings, like the Illinois Regional Library, combine a strict attention to form with a light wit. The observer is encouraged to read the building on two levels: purely architecturally and on a separate narrative level that seems to comment, as from a distance, on the building's program.

16. Frank Norris, *The Pit* (New York, 1956), p. 23.

17. Norman Mailer, *Miami and the Siege of Chicago* (New York, 1968), p. 86.

18. Saul Bellow, *Dangling Man* (New York, 1974), p. 153.

19. See my "Chicago Architecture After Mies," *Critical Inquiry* 6, no. 2 (Winter 1979): 271-89.

20. Stuart E. Cohen, *Chicago Architects* (Chicago, 1976).

21. This rejection of system is not true of the first generation of Miesian critics in Chicago: Bertrand Goldberg, Walter Netsch and Harry Weese. Each doggedly pursued a method or ideology as if to justify their seriousness to Mies, even in protest.

22. Tigerman's spirited and protracted attack on Mies, including a "letter" to Mies ten years after his death and a photo-collage depicting the sinking of Crown Hall like a wounded battleship, indicates a larger rebellion against the "masters." I feel it includes Tigerman's lack of patience with Paul Rudolph, Louis Kahn and John Hejduk

as well, architects with whom he has had a pupil/teacher relationship because of their doctrinaire advocacy of a single architectural system. Tigerman is by habit dialectical in his thought. For every set way of solving a problem he is quick to produce its opposite. In fact, his architecture is most convincing when he holds thesis and antithesis in apocalyptic opposition—admitting of no simple resolution.

23. Some of Tigerman's recent built work admits of some of this same energy. Sam's Cut-Rate Liquor Store is projected to stand in a blasted neighborhood like a Hollywood saloon, complete with false front, riding the movie backlot. By seizing on this theatrical quality he enlivens a rather dreary or straightforward commission. The same energy operates in the ironic facade and plan for the Anti-Cruelty Society where subtle jarring of classic symmetries prepares the visitor for a building serving the two deeply conflicted goals of shelter and, inevitably, of euthanasia.

24. Mailer continues in *Miami and the Siege of Chicago* pp. 89-90. "Yes, Chicago was a town where nobody could ever forget how the money was made. It was picked up from floors still slippery with blood, and if one did not protest and take a vow of vegetables, one knew at least that life was hard, life was in the flesh and the massacre of the flesh—one breathed the last agonies of beasts. So something of the entrails and the secrets of the gut got into the faces of native Chicagoans. A great city, a strong city with faces tough as leather hide and pavement, it was also a city where the faces took on the broad beastiness of ears which were dull enough to ignore the bleatings of the doomed."

25. In many ways Post-Modernism is a rearguard move to recapture some of the "vulgar" energy of the vernacular style. Only the icons have changed. Classical images replace the plastic figures and neon signs. It can also be seen as a dishonest response to the sad nature of contemporary building materials. Gyp board can never imply the solidity of classical materials even if it fools the viewer into a confusion of forms. The dilemma of Post-Modernism is that it is too scholastic and self-conscious to be vulgar enough to be fun and too much a shadow of the real thing to be thought serious.

The Client Doctrine: A Revival of Content

by Dorothy Metzger Habel

In a brief discussion concerning method at the end of *American Architecture and Urbanism,* Vincent Scully remarked that the art historian demands value.[1] What is of value in what is built undoubtedly changes over time, but one possible measure of value in architecture that seems particularly relevant to this historian is the comparative importance placed on the client or user. That Stanley Tigerman should emphasize here his notion of architecture as a matter of service, as something in the service of the client, is especially stimulating in a period characterized by a heavy architectural jive that leaves the layman with a feeling of being peripheral to architecture as well as intellectually outclassed by the architect. Tigerman can jive with the best of them,[2] but he can banter with the client as well. Since 1974, his work has become decidedly bifocal, a fact of which he is fully aware although he prefers to see this as symptomatic of an advanced case of architectural schizophrenia.

In his Introduction to this book, Tigerman addresses the question of whether the architect is the molder of times—the maker and perfecter of times—or merely the reflector and recorder of his age. The question is rhetorical in a sense. There is no doubt in Tigerman's mind that he is a reflector. But the question is also moot; it is far more important to Stanley Tigerman than it is to us. More to the point are the questions of morality and legitimacy. A concern with legitimacy is consistent throughout Tigerman's career and seems to have provoked his client orientation.

Throughout the twentieth century the viewer has been perpetually relegated to a passive role in terms of the art experience regardless of the medium. In architecture this is nowhere more apparent than in the tyranny of Mies van der Rohe and the Modern philosophy in postwar Chicago. Client and citizen participation in the process of architecture was unheard of because it was entirely unnecessary, even irrelevant. If initially wooed by this approach, Tigerman has worked with dogged determination to break with it and to emphasize in his work a sense of process and of client involvement.

In architecture as in no other medium the intersection of artist and viewer is critical. What Tigerman has done with increasing success since 1974 is to force the question: Why do clients turn to architects? The question is simple, but the answer is not always obvious. Clearly the architect is considered a catalyst, an idea man who is enlisted to personalize the assigned program. He is to produce the building or environment, but he is also expected to be an artist. As such, he is encouraged to image the environment and in so doing also produce the unexpected. In the end, he is to create something appealing that goes beyond the client's initial expectations.

In upgrading the role of the client, Tigerman has also given him greater responsibility for the end product. The new importance of the client, and by association the visitor as well, seems a significant revival of his more traditional role throughout history. In Tigerman's recent work the role of the architect is primarily that of form- and image-maker while the content is a collective product reflecting the contemporary world of the client. Through this new matrix of relationships Stanley Tigerman has arrived at his own sense of what is moral and legitimate, at least in his architecture.

Given the attention he has paid to the problem of the house throughout his career, it seems most appropriate to begin an investigation of Tigerman's work with his single-family house. He has designed close to forty domestic projects; of these, well over half have been built. Beginning in the early 1970s, Tigerman seems to attack the house problem with a new energy and enthusiasm. With the designs for Frog Hollow (1973–74) and the Hot Dog House (1974–75) the client enters the program with a startling effectiveness. In the case of Frog Hollow, a barn remodeling project, the possessions of the clients (a grand movie house organ) and their interests in crafts, wild life and the out-of-doors seem ready sources for the materials and forms. There is even a hint of tongue-in-cheek iconographic signification in the cutout fenestration on the black shingle-sided exterior and the provocative mystery of the organ enshrined in the deep pit of the interior.

Shortly after the completion of Frog Hollow, Tigerman announced with almost blasphemous delight that he had done his last serious building.[3] The irony is that at precisely the same time his architecture became most significant. The Hot Dog House, which was in process at that time, has received considerable attention because of its shape—at once pedestrian and whimsically novel. The shape and the simple plan it encases, in fact, reflect the loose and casual weekend life it houses. But there is also the more subtle and satisfying idea of the figure-ground relationship, the orchard screen and closed entrance facade (this becomes the garden facade as well) and the fully fenestrated pond facade now further embellished by the curly screened porch addition. The gentle tensions between the silly built forms and the more finely tuned and intellectual handling of the problems of siting and of front and back add a dimension equal in importance to the client with the provision of a place to "flop."

The first full-blown statement of the collaborative role of the client is the Daisy House (1976–78). The house has been discussed in detail elsewhere, and yet the role of the client in the emotional content has been entirely ignored.[4] The client, in this case an older gentleman diagnosed as terminally ill, is the catalyst for this highly provocative design. The need to amuse the client in the face of a grim situation is a controlling priority, which is covertly demonstrated in the sexual overtones of the plan and deliberately celebrated in the siting of the house—among the Indiana sand dunes overlooking Lake Michigan—and in the sensuous handling of the spaces, surfaces and details. The design hovers between the ribald and the refined. While the suggestively anatomical shapes of the plan control the graphics for the project, they are not terribly apparent to the visitor. Rather, one is struck by the more generic sensuality of the heavy undulating entrance

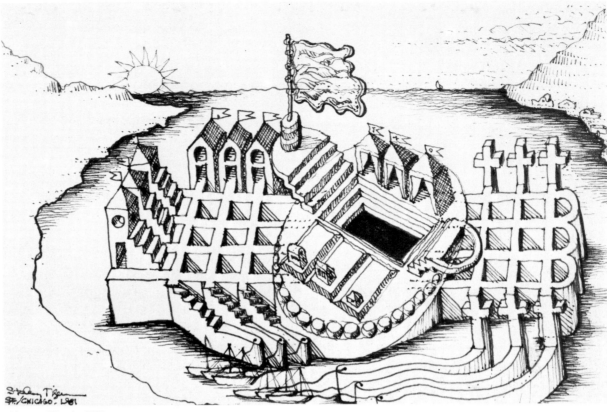

Chicago, Illinois, 1981

facade and the flat and thin lake front so delicately carved by the curving central windows that dance with reflections of the lake. The lake facade is a screen, wider and taller than the building behind, and functions as the major ornament of the house. It becomes a vertical plane that generalizes the more deliberate, if less noticeable, pornography of the plan.

In terms of the more pedestrian problem of the suburban tract house, Tigerman has produced two major designs: Animal Crackers (1976–78) and the Marion House (1978–79). Of these, Animal Crackers is the more noteworthy, although in both cases budget and site limitations as well as the design problem itself eliminated the possibility of solutions as dramatic as Daisy House.[5] And yet the role of the client is a bit less spectacular but no less important. Animal Crackers is a whimsical play on the cracker-box fare of American suburbia. The design is derived from the more stylish and specific logo of the circus wagon immortalized by the Animal Crackers package. Given free reign, the architect would have driven the metaphor further still, painting the cedar siding of the exterior in gay reds and blues accented with gold trim for the hardware. A team of prancing topiary horses was projected to line the short driveway, completing the wagon image. In fact, the restrained program as built seems more effective. The metaphor is considerably subtler and more appropriate to the client's interest in the suburban house program, on the one hand, and in owning a distinctive home on the other.[6]

The house appears more monumental than the average subdivision home because of its chunky proportions and its curved roof line. Something of the circus spectacle remains in the ornamental roof line and the playful fenestration, while a sense of the wagon image is latent in the shape of the whole and its placement on the site. The house, which sits squarely on a perfectly level corner lot in a thin grove of trees, appears to have been left by chance, rather like a great float abandoned on a vacant lot. Once inside, the spaces are

177

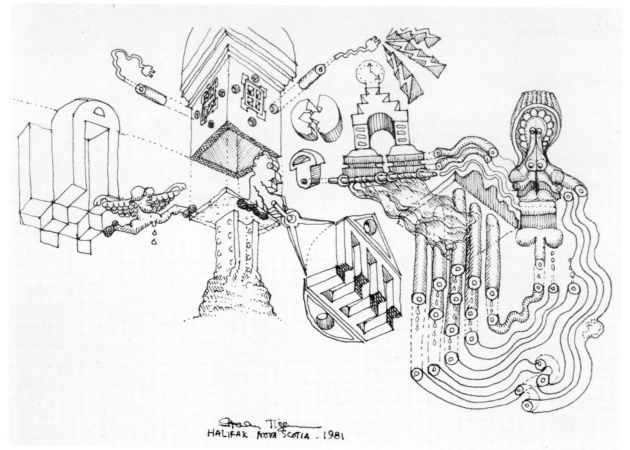

HALIFAX NOVA SCOTIA . 1981

Halifax, Nova Scotia, 1981

varied—some high, some low—according to function. The juxtaposition of spaces of different heights allows for the use of interior fenestration. Lights in the upper story give onto the atriumlike living room of the ground floor. The sense of interior volume is heightened by these irregular and unexpected vistas from one interior space into another above or below. Views to the exterior are framed by the fanciful window shapes. Repetitions of rectangular lights are interspersed with custom-designed curvilinear windows that are rotated and vaguely reminiscent in their shape of the top of a grand piano. The combination of these shapes provides for fragmented and disjointed views to the surrounding, regularized environment of the subdivision. In the end, Animal Crackers is distinct and individual yet also accommodating to the predictable and common setting of suburbia.

Tigerman's adjustment of his architectural style and lan-

guage to the individual client is particularly apparent in the house addition descriptively titled Tigerman Takes a Bite Out of Keck (1977–78). The addition is diminutive in size, consisting of a total of only five hundred square feet. The program demanded an inventive solution, given the desired location of the added space and the limitations of the site. The design involves an addition of space above the flat roof of the existing structure, a relatively large and plain one-story house designed by George Fred Keck in the mid-1960s. The project was commissioned by a stylish couple hoping to expand the quarters of a roomy but undistinguished master bedroom. The added space is multifunctional allowing for a small desk and work area, a dressing room, exercise area and luxurious bath.

Most remarkable is the fact that there is no attempt to accommodate the addition to the existing house. Tigerman's "bite" is loud and aggressive, appearing as a great clamp grabbing Keck's defenseless, flat box. This menacing juxtaposition is reinforced by the curling facade; by the machine-age materials (mirrored glass and stainless steel mullions); and by the giant leap in scale implied between what in reality is a far larger house and a modest addition. The mechanical theme is further heightened by the decorative use of six large fans that are placed in pairs on opposite sides of the structure and recall the neck terminals of Frankenstein. From the interior the added space is not immediately apparent. It seems to roll obliquely upward at the far end of the bedroom. Access to the upper level is provided by an open spiral stair that disrupts one's orientation sufficiently to free the visitor from the four-square predictability and homey warmth of the Keck house. At the top of the stair a relatively narrow sequence of spaces unfolds, moving from the most public area for bill paying and letter writing to the most private and elaborate area for bathing. The entire project is carried out with a sumptuous and modish High-Tech consistency that seems deliberately crass compared with the simplicity of the original house. But the contradiction between sedate home and kicky addition is one that also characterizes the clients and their neighborhood. The owners are socially aggressive and fashion conscious; the "bite" is, in one sense, the architectural equivalent of designer jeans.

In explaining the project Tigerman has insisted that his thesis is that even the smallest addition or remodeling project is not a "throwaway."[7] But the real point here seems to have very little to do with size. In fact, the small size is designed away and, in its place, slick materials, undulating walls, snakelike railings and sensuous passages from one space to another combine both to customize the addition and to antagonize the original house. In the words of the client, "It's really like a work of art."[8]

The role of the client is readily identifiable in the context of designs for single-family houses. After all, it only makes sense that the client play an active role in a building of which he or she will be the prime user. But if easy to identify, the significance of client participation is also obscured in part by the inherently personal nature of the design problem. In the case of Tigerman's work the emphasis on servicing the client is equally identifiable in his public projects and while considerably fewer of these have been built, it is the public design problem that has stimulated the most cogent expressions of the client and service orientation. The earliest public project that is exemplary in the area of client/user accommodation is the design for the Illinois Regional Library for the Blind (1975–78).[9] The design is a landmark in barrier-free design and exhibits Tigerman's careful and creative rethinking of design for the blind and handicapped. A more recent example is his design for the Anti-Cruelty Society (1977–80).

The Anti-Cruelty Society project actually involves an expansion of the downtown Chicago headquarters of the Society. The project also involves an entire revamping of the Society's public image. The addition is large. The plan is divided in two, with the interior, closed side of the corner site devoted to the hard reality of the Society's work in controlling the population of domestic animals. This side is played down; its grim function of animal destruction is quietly and unobtrusively accommodated. The opposite, or exterior, side of the building is assigned the more positive function of animal rehabilitation and adoption. These are the areas that are most visible and accessible to visitors. This division of function is revolutionary in this type of building. In general, animal shelters are depressing facilities in which the functions of destruction and adoption are simultaneously apparent to the visitor. Tigerman's design is controlled in large part by a recognition of the important distinction between these two contradictory operations. The disturbing and sordid is de-emphasized and replaced by an upbeat emphasis on adoption and revival.

The cheery and positive aspects are reinforced by the design of the main facade on North La Salle Street. The facade is symmetrical for the most part, but the dual function of the Society is also revealed. The design of the central section is based on a doggie face; the main entrance resembles the nose and mouth complete with a panting-tongue walk. Curvilinear windows to either side recall the cheeks and jowls, while the inventive triangular cutout pediment—eyes and forehead—completes the canine metaphor. The effect is comical and cute. The left side of the facade, which screens the destructive facilities, is straight and continues the facade line established by the entrance bay. The right side of the facade, however, is controlled by a setback providing a series of shop windows. These wrap around the corner and continue down the side facade. The windows are for displaying the animals ready for adoption. Furthermore, the doggie-in-the-window theme is carefully coordinated with the busy corner bus stop. The open corner at street level and the continuous fenestration above imply a sunny environment for the rehabilitated animals. In all, the sense is of a healthy and clean environment that rids the pets of the stigma of having been stray or abused animals, while the disturbing atmosphere of death and destruction is entirely removed from the public experience.

The design will surely prompt a revision in the image of animal shelters as the grim end for stray and abused pets. In turn, the revised public image will ease the problems of reintegrating the animals into suitable homes. While the design problem may not seem comparable in significance to the Library for the Blind, the close attention to the client's problems and public image as well as to the quality of the experience (for man and beast) in Tigerman's Anti-Cruelty project promises to revolutionize this type of public facility.

In the area of multiple-unit housing, there are two controlling projects, both in Chicago—Boardwalk (1971–74) and Pensacola Place II (1978–81), a companion project. Together, as well as in the context of the rest of Tigerman's work, these two projects demonstrate the kind of stylistic inconsistencies and formal shifts that have annoyed some of his colleagues and nearly all of the critics.[10] In fact, the two function didactically in tandem. Boardwalk is a rectangular, twenty-eight-story apartment tower with a landscaped commercial deck that is, in a work, Miesian.[11] As Tigerman admits, the design is a "rip-off" of the Miesian idiom which by the early 1970s had become so thoroughly ingested as to be more appropriately dubbed the "Chicago" idiom.[12] Entirely predictable and unimaginative, the project was to provide relatively dense middle-income housing on the near North Side. Alone, the building seems a disappointing contribution, especially to the city of Chicago.

The design for Pensacola II appears in large part motivated by the need to rescue Boardwalk as well as the immediate area from the doom cast by the earlier design. Deliverance takes the form of a more complex and exciting high-rise apartment building that is quite literally a Janus piece. Pensacola II is at once a companion piece repeating the original forms of Boardwalk and an alternative to that idiom. The combination of opposing designs is dramatic.

The two major facades are each assigned a different profile. The freeway facade repeats the basic design of the earlier building; the neighborhood facade, or flip side, which is articulated with an applied pseudo-Ionic order and entablature, announces a revised solution to the design problem of the urban apartment tower.

In this case the client of both buildings is the same individual developer. But by virtue of the public nature of the projects and the fact that the client is not the active user of the buildings, the role of the client can be expanded to include the users, the neighborhood and, indeed, the city's public. Even with this unwieldy mix, Tigerman has attacked the business of service with determination. As an ensemble, the buildings demonstrate a contextual commitment to the city. The initial commitment of Boardwalk seems questionable, although it might well be argued (as Tigerman does) that it is, at the very least, consistent with the city fabric.[13] In the end the design seems delinquent in its derivative and mindless motivation. But in expanding the program with the addition of Pensacola II, the scheme is injected with a giant dose of commitment and content. The attention to context is serious and couched in a sophisticated multiplicity. The duality of the Pensacola II facades and the consequent recognition of the past forms and of their influence over the description of the contemporary flip side provokes a varied and rich statement directed to the users and the public about the architectural history of their city. The building functions didactically to demonstrate the historical context and evolution of American urban architecture in general, and of Chicago's unique role in that history in particular.

This bold commitment to content is startling. The questions of history that are forced in the newly established relationship between Boardwalk and Pensacola II are not remarkable for their novelty; they are not new. What is remarkable is that these ideas and questions are couched in terms of built architecture rather than merely in the form of exhibitions or rhetoric. The preferred vehicle in recent years has been graphic or written work, which, although encouraging some degree of public education, has remained fundamentally the creative turf of professional and academic architects.[14] Tigerman himself has helped to establish this more conceptual approach.[15] Most exciting of all is that he has begun to incorporate these concepts into the projects that are built. This transfer to the built environment is a tribute not only to Tigerman but also to his city. Indeed one wonders if this kind of pedagogical statement could be made successfully in any other American city. Chicagoans have been treated to public education in architecture since the late nineteenth century. In this respect, as well, Tigerman's design solution for Pensacola II is tailored to his city's public. Although this is only a brief review of some of Tigerman's relatively recent private and public works, the attention to the client and his role in establishing the design program is a consistent theme. The notion is not so much that of the client controlling the function of a given building as that of the client playing a decisive role in describing the emotional content. The doctrinaire and principled methods and style of the Modern era provide a ready foil to Tigerman's approach and it is one especially relevant given his early background. The Modern doctrine was based on the consistent application of design principles. There were few variables, and the client was certainly not among them. In a sense, Tigerman's concern with legitimacy and morality in architecture seems rooted in a basic distrust of the very period out of which he emerged. For Tigerman the client orientation has become the antidote to the repetitious and inhumane approach of Modern architecture; it has become his own principle or doctrine.

Once recognized, the client doctrine forces some weighty critical questions. First of all, it reveals the contradictory nature of Tigerman's own review of his career. For purposes of this biographical study, Tigerman divides his career into nine phases, which he describes as "nine rather different careers."[16] The divisions are disturbing in as much as they are based solely on matters of style; this is underscored by the assigned labels.[17] In short, the architect himself, while establishing the client as primary, seems to deny the fact that this kind of orientation will inevitably lead to a diversity of styles that are not always consistent. In part the phases do operate chronologically to describe Tigerman's career, but once the client principle is resolved (around Chapter 5) the analytic device of phases becomes contradictory and inappropriate. To assign a determining role to the matter of style seems a serious lapse in the logic of the client resolution itself.

The multiplicity of styles also introduces the question of eclecticism. In no way has Tigerman cornered the market on the eclectic. To be sure the question is receiving more and more attention in the Post-Modern period. But it might be argued, at least in this specific case, that eclecticism—the production of works in more than one style or the combination of various styles in one work—has often gone hand in hand with a client orientation. Consider the variety of designs offered by Christopher Wren for the rebuilding of St. Paul's Cathedral in London or the two styles suggested by Benjamin Latrobe for the Catholic Cathedral in Baltimore. In each case the provision of a choice, of something that strikes the taste and fancy of the patron, seems the prime motive for such bold reversals and apparent contradictions in style. So, too, is the case with Tigerman's work. As a reflector of times, he is challenged to adopt forms that will best suit the client at hand. The dismay this eclecticism has caused seems another residual of the Modern period. In truth, the alarm seems unwarranted. Tigerman's solutions are refreshing; they are tailor-made and strike a decidedly positive chord against the self-indulgent solos of the Modern past.

The question of eclecticism also introduces the matter of the recent revival of interest in the architectural forms of the past. The forms, if not the styles, of the past are reappearing in newly invented contexts. The sources for these motifs range from Peruzzi to Giulio Romano to Palladio, Ledoux and Lutyens. No one period or formal vocabulary is dominant. But at the same time the revival is selective.

This seemingly random adoption of isolated forms from the past, while especially exciting to the historian, is also cause for concern. There is something fundamentally disturbing about this pick-and-choose approach to the formal elements of past programs. The original motives of content are obliterated. In short, the initial relationship of form to content is lost. While it is hard, if not impossible, to exempt Tigerman from this formal criticism, it does seem that he is also involved with a revival that goes beyond the mere reincarnation of forms. Indeed, his most successful projects are those in which the revival of the history of architecture is not in the area of forms but in the area of content, specifically in the area of client involvement.

It is primarily this revival of a traditional approach to content as a collective product of architect and client that recommends Tigerman's recent work. Surely the rediscovery of the lost role of the client is of far greater value than all the elaborate and often obscure references to past forms alone; for in the end this demonstrates a significant revival of the fundamental traditions of humanism in the post-Albertian era.

1. Vincent Scully, *American Architecture and Urbanism* (New York, 1969), p. 257.

2. See, for example, Tigerman's introductory paragraph to his essay for the *Late Entries* exhibition catalog which ends with this statement: "The 'Heroic Phase of Modern Architecture' is over, its leaders are gone, and yet there already exists a sycophantic orthodoxy preparing for their deification ceremonies." Stanley Tigerman, *Chicago Tribune Tower Competition and Late Entries*, 2 vols. (New York, 1980), II, p. 10.

3. Tigerman's statement ("This is my last serious project") is recorded in a review of the Metal and Glass House by Suzanne Philips, which appeared in *Progressive Architecture* 57 (August 1976): 42.

4. Ross Miller, "Stanley Tigerman's Daisy House and Illinois Regional Library — An Architecture of Irony and Distance," *a + u* 11 (November 1979): 109-16.

5. Marion House is a rather different type of solution to the suburban house problem; it is not metaphorical but exclusively formal in its orientation. Tigerman himself describes it as "a warping of the bi-nuclear organization of the International Style." See Lance Knobel, "Recent Work of the Chicago 7," *Architectural Review* 157 (June 1980): 367.

6. For some sense of the client demands and reactions, see "Architectural Surprise: Throwing a Curve," *House & Garden*, 152, no. 8 (August 1980): 96-101.

7. "Walner House—Addition," *a + u* 12 (July 1980): 58.

8. The comment was made in a discussion with the client in September, 1980.

9. Nory Miller, "Illinois Regional Library, Chicago: Fanciful and Functional," *Progressive Architecture* 59 (April 1978): 76-81; Ross Miller, "Stanley Tigerman's Daisy House and Illinois Regional Library," pp. 116-20; and "Beyond Scale: Two Projects for the Physically Handicapped," *Design Quarterly*, 105 (Issues in Architecture, 4).

10. See, for example, Nory Miller, "Illinois Regional Library," p. 76.

11. Boardwalk is discussed in Mildred Floyd Schmertz, "Weese (Ben) versus Mies (Tigerman): Two Buildings, Two Architects, Two Points of View," *Architectural Record* 157 (April 1975): 83-90. The building is also included in Oswald W. Grube, Peter C. Pran and Franz Schulze, *100 Years of Architecture in Chicago* (Chicago, 1977), p. 132.

12. See above, Chapter 1.

13. Ibid.

14. The emergence of Post-Modernism seems to be grounded in large part in the appearance of numerous publications and exhibitions. The appearance of Robert Venturi's *Complexity and Contradiction in Architecture* (New York, 1966) appears to have opened the way for other publications, among them Robert A. M. Stern, *New Directions in American Architecture* (New York, 1969); Peter Blake, *Form Follows Fiasco* (Boston, 1974); B. Brolin, *The Failure of Modern Architecture* (New York, 1976); and Charles Jencks, *The Language of Post-Modern Architecture* (London, 1977). Architectural exhibitions have also proven to be important opportunities for demonstrating the relationship between contemporary and Modern architecture. Among these, the most noteworthy include *Five Architects* (New York, 1972) which was not an exhibition in the strict sense, but rather a major group statement in published form; "Chicago Seven," Richard Gray Gallery, Chicago, December, 1976; and "Transformations in Modern Architecture," Museum of Modern Art, New York, February, 1979.

15. Tigerman has been instrumental in establishing the Chicago Seven, in organizing the "American Architectural Alternatives" exhibition which toured Europe in 1979–1980 and, most recently, in assembling the "Late Entries to the Chicago Tribune Tower Competition," which opened at the Museum of Contemporary Art, Chicago, in May, 1980.

16. See above, Introduction.

17. In general, the division of the work into these nine phases is problematic. There seems to be some confusion as to which projects belong in which categories. For example, I wonder about the inclusion of The Titanic in Chapter 1, the Mies van der Rohe-Influenced, Chicago-School Contextual Phase. It would seem more appropriately placed in Chapter 8, the Historically Allusive Phase, inasmuch as its major thesis is literally the sinking of the Miesian idiom. Similarly, Pensacola II might best fit this phase as well; its historical content seems considerably more important than the irony. These are perhaps picky points, but they do demonstrate something of the fallacy inherent in the use of stylistic divisions.

List of Projects

Page numbers refer to pages on which illustrations appear.

Three: Geometric/Megastructure Phase 1958–1972

Four: Advocacy/Socially Conscious Phase 1963–1978

Five: Manipulated Modernist Phase 1971–1981

Six: Surrealist Phase 1969–1979

Bibliography

Architectural League of New York. *John Hejduk*. New York, 1967. Exhibition catalogue.

Arieti, Silvano. *Abraham and the Contemporary Mind*. New York, 1981.

———. *Creativity: The Magic Synthesis*. New York, 1976.

Birnbaum, Philip, ed. and trans. *The Concise Jewish Bible: A New Translation*. New York, 1976.

Blaser, Werner. *Mies van der Rohe: The Art of Structure*. New York, 1965.

Boman, Thorleif. *Hebrew Thought Compared with Greek*. rev. ed. Translated by Jules L. Moreau. New York, 1970.

Bourgoin, J. *Les Éléments de l'art Arabe*. Paris, 1879.

Bucher, François. *Josef Albers: Despite Straight Lines*. New Haven, 1961.

Ciucci, Giorgio; Dal Co, Francesco; Manieri-Elia, Mario; and Tafuri, Manfredo. *The American City: From the Civil War to the New Deal*. Translated by Barbara Luigia. Cambridge, Mass., 1979.

Dobschutz, E. von. "Zeit und Raum." *Journal of Biblical Literature* 16 (1922).

Dunster, David, ed. *Michael Graves*. New York, 1979.

Eliade, Mircea. *The Sacred and the Profane: The Nature of Religion*. Translated by Willard R. Trask. New York, 1957.

Fletcher, Sir Bannister. *A History of Architecture on the Comparative Method*. 18th rev. ed. New York, 1975.

Fondation Corbusier. *John Hejduk*. Paris, 1972. Exhibition catalogue.

Giedion, Sigfried. *Space, Time and Architecture: The Growth of a New Tradition.* 5th rev. ed. Cambridge, Mass., 1967.

Goldin, Judah, ed. and trans. *The Living Talmud: The Wisdom of the Fathers and Its Classical Commentaries.* New Haven, 1955.

Hersey, George L. *Pythagorean Palaces: Magic and Architecture in the Italian Renaissance.* Ithaca, N.Y., 1976.

Hilbert, David, and Cohn-Vossen, S. *Geometry and the Imagination.* Translated by P. Nemenyi. New York, 1952.

Hubben, William. *Dostoevsky, Kierkegaard, Nietzsche and Kafka: Four Prophets of Our Destiny.* 9th rev. ed. New York, 1979.

Jaffé, H.L.C. *De Stijl, 1917–1931.* J. M. Meulenhoff, Amsterdam, 1956. Exhibition catalogue.

Loerke, William C. "Observations on the Representation of Doxa in the Mosaics of S. Maria Maggiore, Rome, and St. Catherine's, Sinai." *Gesta* 20/1 (1981).

Luckiesh, Mathew. *Visual Illusions: Their Causes, Characteristics and Applications.* 1922. Reprint. New York, 1965.

Martin, J. L.; Nicholson, Ben; and Gabo, N.; eds. *Circle: International Survey of Constructive Art.* New York, 1971.

Munari, Bruno. *Discovery of the Square.* New York, 1965.

Nygren, Anders. *Agape and Eros: A Study of the Christian Idea of Love.* 1932. Reprint. Translated by Philip S. Watson. Chicago, 1982.

Rowe, Colin, and Slutzky, Robert. "Transparency: Literal and Phenomenal." *Perspecta* 8 (1963): 45-54.

Rykwert, Joseph. *On Adam's House in Paradise: The Idea of the Primitive Hut in Architectural History.* New York, 1972.

Scholem, Gershom. *On the Kabbalah and Its Symbolism.* Translated by Ralph Manheim. New York, 1965.

Schwarz, Rudolph. *The Church Incarnate: The Sacred Function of Christian Architecture.* Chicago, 1958.

Seuphor, Michel. *Piet Mondrian: Life and Work.* New York, (n. d.).

Spencer, John R., ed. and trans. *Leon Battista Alberti on Painting.* rev. ed. New Haven, 1966.

Stedelijk Museum. *De Stijl: Catalogue #81.* Amsterdam, 1951. Exhibition catalogue.

Steinsaltz, Adin. *The Essential Talmud.* New York, 1976.

Stern, Robert A. M. "Yale 1950–1960." *Oppositions* 4: 35-62.

Summerson, Sir John. *Heavenly Mansions and Other Essays on Architecture.* New York, 1963.

Wagner, Roy. *The Invention of Culture.* rev. ed. Chicago, 1981.

Watkin, David. *Morality and Architecture: The Development of a Theme in Architectural History and Theory from the Gothic Revival to the Modern Movement.* Oxford, 1977.

Acknowledgments

The embryonic notion for this book came as a result of criticism I received from the Palladian scholar James Ackerman following a lecture I delivered in 1980 when I was at the American Academy in Rome. I had combined a slide show of my work with theories about Jeffersonian-brand democracy, quoting Emerson, Whitman and Thoreau in the process. Professor Ackerman criticized this juxtaposition, pointing out that while my work had little in common with eighteenth and nineteenth-century American concepts it had a great deal to do with the America of my own times and he suggested that I verbalize the ideas embodied in my architectural projects.

After I had clarified my attitudes about post-Viet Nam America, I began to test these ideas on the American architectural lecture circuit. An early respondent was the architectural journalist Nory Miller who corresponded with me about dualist thought in terms of architectural analysis. Professor Thomas Schumacher of the University of Virginia offered insights into aspects of Judaism I had not connected with architecture, Professor William Loerke of Dumbarton Oaks generously shared his innovative essay about Hellenic and Hebraic concerns and Professor Ackerman of Harvard University gave me access to his unpublished paper positing a theory of art criticism. The architectural critic Olivier Bois-sière made invaluable textual suggestions.

The opportunity to examine many of the concepts I was developing took place during sessions of my architectural theory course at the University of Illinois at Chicago Circle. Darcy Bonner, Virginia Greene and Robert Krone were among the graduate students who helped to enrich my thoughts through argumentation and analysis. I am indebted to Caren Redish and Deborah Doyle for the many discussions conducted on the subject of wit, humor and irony in architecture without which Chapter 7 (Architecture of the Absurd) would be only partially fleshed out.

I wish to thank Professors Ross Miller of the University of Connecticut and Dorothy Metzger Habel of the University of Tennessee for their evaluative essays as presented in the context of the particular positions they separately took.

I am grateful to Rizzoli International Publications, in particular to Gianfranco Monacelli, William Dworkin and John Brancati. I am indebted to my editor, Brenda Gilchrist, for her patience during this endurance contest. Without the tenacity of my secretary, Dianne Sancya, through the several manuscript drafts, none of this would have been possible, and I would like to acknowledge Susan Grant Lewin for her help in the selection of the title. Finally, I wish to thank my forbearing wife, Margaret McCurry, whose determination for clarity pulled me, yelling and screaming, into this naked state.